NAMES OF PERSONS

WHO TOOK THE

Oath of Allegiance to the State of Pennsylvania,

BETWEEN THE YEARS 1777 AND 1789,

WITH

A HISTORY OF THE "TEST LAWS" OF PENNSYLVANIA.

BY

THOMPSON WESTCOTT.

PHILADELPHIA:
JOHN CAMPBELL.
MDCCCLXV.

Notice

In many older books, foxing (or discoloration) occurs and, in some instances, print lightens with wear and age. Reprinted books, such as this, often duplicate these flaws, notwithstanding efforts to reduce or eliminate them. The pages of this reprint have been digitally enhanced and, where possible, the flaws eliminated in order to provide clarity of content and a pleasant reading experience.

Originally published
Philadelphia
1865

Reprinted by:

Janaway Publishing, Inc.
732 Kelsey Ct.
Santa Maria, California 93454
(805) 925-1038
www.janawaygenealogy.com

2010

ISBN 10: 1-59641-222-4
ISBN 13: 978-1-59641-222-4

Made in the United States of America

HISTORY

OF THE

"TEST LAWS" OF PENNSYLVANIA.

FIRST BOOK.

We whose names are hereunto Subscribed Do solemnly and sincerely Declare and Swear, (or affirm,) That the State of Pensilvania is and of right ought to be a free Sovereign and Independent State—and I do forever renounce all Allegiance, Subjection and Obedience to the King or Crown of Great Britain, and I do further swear (or solemnly, sincerely and truely declare and affirm) that I never have since the declaration of Independence, directly or Indirectly aided, assisted, abetted or in any wise countenanced the King of Great Britain, his Generals, fleets or armies; or their adherents in their claims upon these United States, and that I have ever since the declaration of the Independence thereof demeaned myself as a faithfull citizen and subject of this or some one of the United States, and that I will at all times maintain and support the freedom, sovereignty and Independence thereof.

1778.
Decr. 11, HENRY SCHWALBAH.
    12, BENJAMIN LOXLY, JUNR., late a prisoner in Europe.
    14, DAVID JONES, Farmer.
    15, JOHN CROWDEN (his mark), of Philada., Labourer.
        JOHN WEYANT.
    16, JOHN STONE.
        ADAM HUBLEY, of Philada., Mercht.
        JACOB HARMAN, of Philada., Mercht. Affirmed.
        JAMES McGILL (his mark), do. Labourer.

1778.
Decr. 18, JOHN NIXON, ⎫
  J. M. NESBITT, ⎬ Auditors of Accounts.
  BENJ. FULLER, ⎭
  BARTHOLOMEW MOORE, Mariner, lately in the State fleet.
 19, ABRAHAM LEVERING, Roxborough. Affirmed.
  JACOB GILBERT, JUNR.
  JACOB GILBERT, the elder.
  CASPAR SAUDER.
 21, MICHAEL ORNER, Labourer.
  ANDREW BRAND, Grocer.
  LEONARD KROMER, Northern Liberties.
  EVERHART GEISS (his mark), Northern Liberties.
  JOHN RIGHTER, Roxborough.
 22, BENJAMIN PASCHALL, ESQ. Affirmed.
  ROBERT JEWELL. Affirmed.
  CHARLES BOWER, sworn Dec. 24th.
  JOSEPH REED, President of the Executive Council.
  GEORGE BRYAN, Vice President.
  JOSEPH HART, ⎫
  JOHN MACKY, ⎪
  MATTHEW SMITH, ⎬ Members of the Supreme Executive Council.
  JAMES READ, ⎪
  JACOB ARNDT, ⎪
  THOMAS SCOTT, ⎭
  TIMOTHY MATLACK, Secy. of the Council. Affirmed.
 25, DANIEL RIGHTER, Roxborough.
  MICHAEL RIGHTER, do.
  JOHN RIGHTER, do.
  JAMES HORNER, of Philada., Sadler.

1778.
Decr. 27, JOSEPH STRETCH, of Philada., Mercht. Affirmed.
    SAMUEL LANGDALE, do. do. do.
    GEORGE CHANDLER, of do. Escort. do.
    WILLIAM MATLACK, do. Watchmaker. do.
  28, ANDREW DOZ, Philada., Gent.
  30, JACOB CONRAD, JR. (his mark), Lower Merrion.
1779.
Jan. 1, FREDERICK SEEGEZ, Shopkeeper.
    SAMUEL LYON, Commissary.
    JAMES DUNLAP, Philada., Physician.
  2, PETER CRISPIN, Roxbury.
    JOHN TIBIN, JR., do.
    JOSEPH LEAMAN (his mark), do.
    MICHAEL SMITH (his mark), Merrion. Farmer.
    WILLIAM KIDD, Schoolmaster.
  4, PHILIP RUMBLE (his mark), Labourer.
    MICHAEL METZINGER (his mark), Weaver.
  5, NICHOLAS JACOBS, Cordwainer.
    WILLIAM LAWRENCE, Hatter. Affirmed.
    PHILIP TRUCKENMILLER, Taylor.
    JONATHAN DRAPER, Cordwainer.
    JOHN GARDNER, do.
    MARTIN BENNER (his mark).
    PETER SUTTER, Hatter.
    GEORGE ATTKINSON, Ship Captain.
    ADAM MYRTELUS, Blacksmith.
    JACOB ERINGER, of Philada., Hosier.
    MILES HILLBORN, Mercht. Affirmed.
    ANDREW TYBOUT, Hatter.
    LEVY MARKS, Taylor.

1779.
Jan. 5, BARNABY DEMPSEY (his mark), Labourer.
    9, JOHN FRY (his mark), of Abbendon.
       JAMES CLAYPOOLE ESQ., High-Sheriff.
       JOHN KEBLE, Clark.
       RICHARD SALTAR, Shipwright.
       THOMAS VAUGHAN,   do.
       NATHANIEL GREEN,   do.
       LEWIS HAZLEWANGER (his mark), do.
       CONRAD LUTZ,   do.
       JOHN MCKIM.
    13, JACOB GRAFF, Philada.
       JACOB BECHER, Lancaster Co.
       JOHN ANDREWS (his mark), Philada., Waterman.
    14, ANDREW MERVINE (his mark), Cooper.
       BENJAMIN LEAVERING (his mark), Cordwainer.
    16, JOHN KELLY, Asst. Bar. Masr., who also took the oath of office.
    18, EDWARD KERAN, of Philada., Scrivener.
    21, JOHN WEAVER, late in the American Military service.
    26, JOSEPH SHRIVER, of Philada., Butcher.
    28, JOHN AMOS, Lower Merrion, Shoemaker.
       JACOB AMOS (his mark), Roxborough.
    29, CHRISTOPHER BAKER.
    30, THOMAS MCDOWELL, of Philada., Soapboiler.
Feb. 3, JOSEPH SELLERS, Kingsessing. Affirmed.
    4, WILLIAM HOLLINSHEAD ESQ.
       WILLIAM ALBRECHT, Philada., Barber.
       WENDELL KINGSFIELD, Lower Merrion.
    10, WILLIAM COCHRAN, L. Merrion.

1779.
Feb. 10, JAMES CHRISTY (his mark), of Bucks, on the publick service.
    13, GEORGE FISHER (his mark), Roxbury.
        JOSEPH PRICE, Carpenter. Affirmed.
    16, JOHN BELL, Shoemaker. Affirmed.
    17, PHILIP SYNG, Gentleman.
    18, GEORGE ROSS ESQ., Judge of Admiralty.
    20, JAMES RUSSELL, of Lower Merrion.
    23, WILLIAM DUNTON, late a prisoner.
        JOHN DANIEL, late of Bucks Co.
    24, JOHN CONNER, in the publick service.
    27, THOMAS CANNAN, Breeches maker.
        JOSEPH KENDALL, Physitian. Affirmed.
        MICHAEL SHUBART ESQ., Member of Assembly.
        JOHANN CONRAD BROWN, of Philada., Cordwainer.
March 1, WILLIAM FULLERTON, Lower Merrion, Taylor.
    9, PHILIP ROTH, of Philada., Musitian.
       BENJAMIN GORGAS, Roxborough.
       JOHN GORGAS,   do.
    10, JACOB SHARP, in the publick service.
       ANDREW SHARP (his mark), in the publick service.
       SAMUEL BAKER, Kensington, Shipwright.
    11, FREDERICK HITNER, of Philada., Tanner.
    12, JOHN LODGE, of Passiunk.
       WILLIAM JONES,
       JOSEPH DURLING, } Mariners of the State of Massachusetts.
       JOHN SMITH,
    13, JACOB AMOS, of Roxborough, Philada. Co.
       JACOB FISLER, of Merrion.
       JOHN HOLEGIT, of Roxborough. Affirmed.

1779.
March 13, ANDREW DAMM, of Philada., Dealer.
    JOHN VESTARD (his mark), of Philada., Brickmaker.
    PETER DAVID HANSIL (his mark), of Kingsessing.
  19, JOHN ROUKING, of Philada.
  20, LAZARUS PINE ESQ., of Philada., Capt. of Militia.
  24, ANDREW FITE, of Roxborough.
  26, WILLIAM WATKINS,
      JONATHAN PAUL,
      WILLIAM DAVIES,
      PHILIP REFFERT,
      JAMES MCCOTTER, } belonging to the Company of Artificers.
      LEONARD EGEN,
      JACOB ALBRIGHT,
      ROBERT IRWIN,
      DAVID PAUL,
    JOHN GEORGE FOX SENR.,   do.
    JOHN HARRAWAY,   do.
  27, THOMAS BOURNE, of Philada., Gentleman.
    JOHN BIGONY (his mark), of Roxborough, Hosier.
    DAVID RITTENHOUSE ESQ., State Treasurer.
    CORNELIUS HOULGATE, of Roxborough. Affirmed.
    JOSEPH BIGONY,   do.
    MATTHEW HOLEGET,   do.   Affirmed.
    JOSEPH STURGIS,   do.   do.
    JACOB LUTCH (his mark), Lower Merrion, Cordwainer.
  29, PETER TAYLOR, of Philada, Carpenter.
    JACOB CONROD (his mark), of Lower Merrion.
    THOMAS NEVELL,
    JACOB SCHREINER, } Street Commissioners.
    JOHN MCCULLOH,

1779.
March 29, GEORGE DUNHOWER (his mark), Kingsessing.
        CHRISTOPHER ELLIOTT, do. Affirmed.
        JOHN FAJON, of Roxborough.
        JOHN WALTERS, Kingsessing.
        ISAAC GRANT, do.
        ROBERT RIGG, of the Company of Carpenters.
        WILLIAM ROSE, do.
    30, WILLIAM CHAIN, of Philada., Tallow Chandler.
        NEELS JONASSON, of Kingsessing.
        FREDERICK HOLSTEN, do.
        MATTHIAS HOLSTEN, do.
        JOHN MATZINGER (his mark), do.
    31, JACOB HAASS, of Philada. Co., of the Co. of Carpenters.
        WILLIAM FIANS, Kingsessing.
        ISRAEL MORTON, do.
        STOKELY HOSSMAN.
        (HON.) JOHN HAMBRIGHT, Mem. of Ex. Council.
        REUBEN HALL, Philada., Carpenter.
        MARTIN MILLER, Lower Merrion. Affirmed.
        JOHN GOODMAN, do. do.
        JACOB CASTER, Oxford.
        HENRY KATZ, Whitemarsh.
        JACOB LAUGHLIN,   ⎫
        GEORGE SCHLOSSER, ⎪
        WILLIAM RUSH,   ⎬ County Assessors.
        CHRISTIAN SCHNEIDER, ⎪
        ROBERT CURRY,   ⎭
        WILLIAM RICHARDS, Asst. Assessor.
        WILLIAM GREENWAY, Measurer of Grain.

1779.
March 31, BENJAMIN PASCHALL, Kingsessing. Affirmed.
    PAUL CONNER, Roxborough. Affirmed.
    RUDOLPH LATCH, Lower Merrion.
    JOSEPH STILES, Commissary of Mil. Stores. Affirmed.
    GEORGE BELL, Darby Township.
    EDWARD PRICE. Affirmed.
    GEORGE MORTON, Kingsessing.
    ABRAHAM HOLMES, Darby.
    SAMUEL TAYLOR, Kingsessing.
    SAMUEL YOUNG, Philada., Carpenter.
    GEORGE JANUS, D. M., Philada.
    ROBERT TOWERS JUNR., Philada., Cutler.
    JOHN HENDERSON, of Philada., Conducr. Mil. Stores.
    CHRISTIAN BEACKLEY, Philada., Supt. Artificers.
    DAVID DAVIES, Comp. Artificers.
    RUDOLPH SIBLEY (his mark), Lower Merrion.
    PETER HOLSTEN, Kingsessing.
    PETER ROSE, Blockley.
    JACOB ROWAND, of Philada., Shoemaker.
    HENRY SHOSTER, Lower Merrion.
    GUNNING BEDFORD, Philada., Carpenter.
    GEORGE GROTZ, of Philada., Breeches Maker.
April 7, (DOCTR.) ALVERY HODGSON, Surgeon Genl. Hospital.
    ROBT. WILSON, late of New Jersey, now of Philada., Mercht.
    JACOB LEVERING, of Roxborough.
13, HENRY MCGEE (his mark), of Philada., Labourer.
14, JOSIAH GILL, of Philada., Shop Keeper. Affirmed.

1779.
April 24, SETH WILLIS, of Philada.
    28, EVAN MORRIS, of Philada., Shoemaker.
    29, JAMES DAVIS, of Merrion, Schoolmaster.
May 4, JOHN DUMFIELD (his mark), a non resident, late of the Jersey State.
    5, JOHN ROBERTS, of Lower Merrion, Farmer. Affirmed.
       SEBASTIEN HOUSHOLD (his mark), a non resident.
    7, ANDREAS FISHER (his mark), of Blockley, Farmer.
    10, THOMAS CARTER, of Philada., Taylor.
    13, THOMAS HALE, Agent for forfeited estates, who also took the oath of said office.
    15, WILLIAM MCSPARRAN, of Philada., Spinner.
       JOHN HORN, of Philada., Spinner.
    22, PETER STOUT, of Philada., Labourer.
       PHILIP CLAUZER (his mark), do. do.
    24, WILHELM FRIEDERICH, of Passyunk, Farmer.
    25, GEORGE YOUNG, of Moyamensing, Farmer.
       HUGH COLVIN (his mark), late of Chester Co., in the publick service.
       ANDREW LEMAU, of Philada., Harness Maker.
       CONRAD SHALLER,
       PHILIP YOUNG,
       HEINRICH LENTZ,
       JOHANNES RITIGER,
} Having renounced allegiance to the English, which they were constrained to take.
    26, BASTIA VENIA (his mark).
       JOSEPH MEYER,
       JACOB KEISLER (his mark),
} Moyamensing Farmers.
    27, (Mr.) P. E. DU SIMITIERE, of Philada., Gentleman.
       LUDWIG TAYLOR, Northern Liberties, Cutter.

1779.
May 27, JOHN DANIEL, of Philada.
JOHN CORBRIGHT, do.
28, JAMES STURGIS, of Blockley, Weaver.
HENRY GIBBONS (his mark), of Philada., Labourer.
29, HENRY THIELL, of Philada., Blacksmith.
31, JOHN YOUNG, lately residing in the Jersey State.
WM. RUSK, of Philada., late Butcher.
ANDREW WAY, of Philada., Taylor.
June 2, GEORG BECHTEL, of Philada., Labourer.
WILLIAM WRIGHT, of Philada., Sailmaker.
3, JOHN MALONE (his mark), of Philada., Taverner and Huxter.
9, VALENTINE HASIG, of Roxbury, Labourer.
12, WILLIAM HANSELL, Philada., Blacksmith.
19, HUGH MITCHELL, Clark to Col. Mitchell.
JOHN MURGATROYD, of Philada., Merchant.
23, HENRY HART (his mark), of the City Watch, took the test in 1777.
GEORGE HART (his mark), of the City Watch, testified in 1777.
JOSEPH HARVEY, late of Bermuda.
WILLIAM SLOAN, of Cranbury, New Jersey.
JAMES THOMPSON, of Essex Co., New Jersey.
July 8, JOHN STARKE, of Philada., Wheelwright. Took the test to the States in 1777 & was constrained to Allegiance to the Brittish.
JOHN BRITTIN, of New Jersey.
30, SAML. CRAWFORD, of Philada., Mariner.
JOHN MCCARTNEY, of Philada., Taylor.
JACOB CHRYSTLER, of Philada., Shopkeeper.

1779.
July 30, EDWARD YOUNG, of Philada., Sadler.
      WILLIAM METAY, of Philada., Sadler.
    31, MATTHEW FOLK,   do.   Skindresser.
      PETER HUTMAN (his mark), of Philada., Chairmaker.
      FRANCIS GEISSE, of Philada., Silversmith, took the test in 1777, was constrained to swear to the Brittish when here.
      AMBROSE CROKER, of Philada.
      JAMES LUCAS, Adjutant in the Artillery of Artificers.
      JOHN THORNHILL JUNR., of Philada., Shoemaker.
Aug. 2, GEORGE SWATS,   of Philada., Taylor.
      HENRY HYNEMAN (his mark), do.   do.
      JOHN LIPPEE (his mark), of Passyunk, Labourer.
      CHRISTIAN CHEVILIER (his mark), do.   do.
      JOHN HAY, of Philada.
      JAMES STEEL, of Philada., Gent.
      ISAAC COURSE,   do.   do.
      CHARLES LOARDAN, took the test in 1777.
      JACOB FACUNDUS, of Philada., Blacksmith.
      DANIEL MORRISON (his mark), of Philada., Labourer.
      JOHN COPPLE (his mark), of Passyunk.
      JOHN BARCLAY,   do.   Mercht.
      JOHN DOUGLASS, of Passyunk, Linen Printer.
      PETER SMALLWOOD (his mark), Shoemaker.
      JACOB STEINMIRES (his mark), of Philada., Shoemaker.
      JOHN COLLINS,   of Philada., Cooper.
      HEINRICH SMALTZ,   do.   Joyner.
      GEORGE IRONRING (his mark), do.   Labourer.
      JOHN MOORE,   do.   Butcher.

1779.

Aug. 2, MICHAEL STANLEY (his mark), of Philada., Cordwainer.
    PEARCE LEWIS, do. do.
    JOHN WYANT, of Northern Liberties, Labourer.
    JOHN WOOD (his mark), do. do.
    GEORGE APT (his mark), do. Pumpmaker.
    JAMES CARUTHERS, of Philada., Shopkeeper.
    CASPER FLEISHER, do. Skinner.
    GEORGE SINK, do. Labourer.
    GEORGE HINEY, of Northern Liberties, Labourer.
    THOMAS BECK (his mark), City of Philada., Cordwainer.
    NICHOLAS HYSMMINGLE, do. Carpenter.
    JOHN RIED (his mark), of Northern Liberties, Baker.
    CHRISTIAN KIRKHOFF, of Philada., Clark.
    ANDREW MCINTIRE, do. Joyner.
    DANIEL SHAW, do. Carpenter.
    GEORGE HESS, do. Smith.
    RICHARD GUY, do. Carpenter.
    ROBERT LEECH, do. do.
    WILLIAM GRIFFITH (his mark), do. Labourer.
    JOHN SPIEGEL, do. Combmaker.
    EDWARD DICKENS, do. Painter.
    JAMES ROTHBOTTOM, do. Bricklayer.
    JOHN GUY, do. Carter.
    JOHN BEAKS, do. Carpenter.
    GODFREY BACKIUS, do. Hatter.
    RICHARD HALL, do. Carpenter.
    ABRAHAM AKELY (his mark), do. Cooper.
    CONRAD PIGEON, do. Bricklayer.

1779.
Aug. 2, PETER BOYLE (his mark), of Philada., Brewer.
JOHN DEAL, do. Labourer.
JOHN KEYS, do. Hatter.
PETER MELLENBERGER (his mark), do. Labourer.
JONATHAN SMITH, Northern Liberties, Carpenter.
JOSEPH SMITH, Northern Liberties, Saddlemaker.
JOSIAH HAZLETON, Northern Liberties, Smith.
WILLIAM THORN, City, Carpenter.
GEORGE TILL, Northern Liberties, Shipwright.
MICHAEL SHILLING (his mark), City, Combmaker.
WILLIAM POWELL, N. Liberties, Sawyer.
RICHARD TAYLOR, Southwark, Mariner.
JOHN ARMSTRONG (his mark), City, Labourer.
HENRY PERRET, City, Soapboiler.
JOHN PARKHILL, City, Gunsmith.
JAMES HUMPHREYS (his mark), N. Liberties, Shipwright.
JOHN RUTHERFORD, of Philada., Currier.
BENJAMIN BOULTER, do. Carpenter.
JOHN RICE, do. Baker.
NICHOLAS GRIM, do. Sawyer.
JOHN WHITEMAN, do. Taylor.
JOHN WAINE (his mark), do. Labourer.
ANDREW ISINHOOT, N. Liberties, Coppersmith.
HUGH FERGUSON, City, Coachman.
PETER GREEN (his mark), N. Liberties, Currier.
ISAAC CAUSTEN, City, Founder.
FREDERICK GRISLER, do. Innholder.
WILLIAM LOHMAN, Passiunk, Farmer.
WILLIAM BUDDEN, Capt., Philada.

1779.
Aug. 2, GEORGE COOK, inlisted in the Regt. of Artificers.
MICHAEL FOX, City, Turner.
JOHN HOFFSTEDLER, City, Cooper.
JACOB MAAG, City, Wheelwright.
SAMUEL STERN, do. Carpenter.
JOHN SHAFER, do. Butcher.
JOHN McNAIR, do. Taylor.
WILLIAM MILLER, do. Printer.
GEORGE STOW, do. Turner.
3, JACOB BOST (his mark), Passiunk, Farmer.
JACOB SMITH (his mark), do. do.
GEORGE MOSER (his mark), Kensington, Smith.
ALEXANDER BARCLAY (his mark), City, Waggoner.
JOHN QUAIN, City, at the Laboratory.
5, JONATHAN CLAY, do. Blacksmith.
GEORGE SCHNEIDER, do. Farmer.
WILLIAM BAKER (his mark), do. Labourer.
6, JOHN ANDERSON, do. Taylor.
7, ADAM GARRETT (his mark), Passiunk, Farmer.
EDWARD CARTWRIGHT, late of Philada., Blacksmith.
9, HENRY SAVETT, of Southwark, Labourer.
10, JOHN McFARLANE, of Philada., late of New York, Mercht.
JACOB BANKSON the Elder, of Southwark, Yeoman.
JAMES TAWNEY, of Philada., Travelling Dealer.
18, NICHOLAS MILLER, of do. Labourer.
19, CARL BLUTZER, a Hessian deserter: oath of June 13, 1777.
20, DAVID CROTTY, Seaman, lately discharged from the State Fleet.

1779.
Aug. 20, JOHAN UMBRIGHT, of Philada., Taylor.
TERENCE DONNELLY, of the State of Connecticut.
MICHAEL MÜLLER, of Southwark, Gun Stocker.
RICHARD LUDGATE (his mark), of Philada., Labourer.
23, JAMES HARRIS, do. Cordwainer.
30, SOLOMON TAYLOR, late of Virginia, Blacksmith.
Sept. 3, JOSEPH WEBB, of Philada., House Carpenter. Affirmed.
4, DAVID HANSELL, of Kingsessing, Farmer.
6, JOHN MILLER (his mark), of Philada., Baker. Affirmed.
ANDREW HODGE JUNR., do. absent in the West Indies until November last.
9, MICHAEL LETTS (his mark), of Whitemarsh, Farmer.
ROBERT MILLER, of the N. Liberties, Labourer.
(CAPT.) JOHN LAWSON, of Philada., Mariner.
11, WILLIAM NOLBROW, do. Taylor.
13, ROBERT CORNISH, do. Sailor.
17, JOHN MILLS (his mark), of the N. Liberties, Labourer.
18, ARTHUR HURRY, of Philada., Taylor, now near 19 yrs. of age.
25, GEORGE SNELING (his mark), of Philada., Weaver.
29, CHARLES LOGAN, do. Mercht. Affirmed.
30, JEAN LOUIS REY, late of Geneva, Mercht.
Oct. 4, JAMES HUDSON, of Philada., Sadler and Harness Maker.
WILLIAM WARNER JUNR., of Blockley.
7, WALTER HALL, of Philada., Merchant.
9, JOHN SOLTER, of Philada., Baker.

1779.

Oct. 9, JESSE JONES, of Lower Merrion Township, Philada. co. Affirmed.

11, JOHN ERDMAN SMITH, of Philada., Printer.
CHARLES MERIDITH, do. Gentleman.
ALGERNON ROBERTS.
WILLIAM JACKSON, of Philada., Mercht.

12, ROBERT HEYSHAM, of do. do.
CHARLES STEDMAN, do. Gentleman.
CARPENTER WHARTON, of Southwark, Mercht.
JOHN KESSLER.
JOHN PALMER, of Philada., Tavern keeper.
PETER LIGHT (his mark), Philada., Labourer.
WILLIAM COLLOM (his mark), worker in the Armory, Philada.

Lists of the foregoing returned to Election at State House.

Oct. 13, WILLIAM JONES, of Philada., Grazier.
GEORGE WALKER, do. Victualer.
ABRAHAM SINK (his mark), do. Brassfounder.
PETER RAMBO, do. Sadler.

14, JOSEPH HILLBORN, do. Mercht. Affirmed.
GEORG DAVID SICKEL, do. Butcher.
JAMES CALDWELL, of Northern Liberties, Labourer.
CHARLES KNIGHT, of Philada., Miller.
JOHN DIAMOND, do. Ropemaker.
JAMES ARMSTRONG, do. Trader.
DANIEL BENEZET, do. Mercht.
JOHN BARE, do. Hatter.

1779.
Oct. 14, SAMUEL PENROSE, of Philada., Mercht.
    15, GEORGE DELANEY, Darby, Seaman.
    16, THOMAS SMITH (his mark), Philada., do.
        JOHN BECK, do. Taylor.
        JOHN WEAVER, do. do.
        JOSHUA JONES, Lower Dublin, Philada. co., Farmer.
        ISAAC WHARTON, of Philada., Mercht. Affirmed.
        CHARLES WHARTON, do. do. do.
        JOSEPH HIBBARD, Blockley, Farmer.
        SAMUEL PETERS, Philada., Schoolmaster.
        JOHN HEFFERNAN, do. do.
        JOHN OTENKERKEN, do. Labourer.
    18, JOHN PORTER, do. Student in Phisick.
        MICHAEL LEIB, do. do.
        JACOB FRANK, do. Silversmith.
        PETER KURTZ, do. Tobacconist.
        GODFREY SHISLER, Passiunk, Farmer.
        JAMES KINNEAR, of Philada., Mercht.
        PETER FOOTMAN, do. do.
        JOHN GROVER, Lower Merrion, Farmer.
        HEINRICH COLFLESH, do. do.
        MATHIAS COLFLESH, do. do.
        JOHANNES WALTERS, do. do.
        PHILIP PRITNER, do. do.
        ISRAEL JONES, do. do. Affirmed.
        THOMAS MORGAN, do. do. Affirmed.
        ROBERT BASS, Philada., Druggist.
        THOMAS GRESWOLD, Northern Liberties. do.

1779.
Oct. 18, JONATHAN ZANE, Northern Liberties, Mercht.
JOHN CARNS JUNR., Darby, Chester Co., Yeoman.
EDWARD ELLIOTT, Philada., Clark.
TENCH FRANCIS, Philada., Gent.
JOSEPH PALMER, do. Mercht. Affirmed.
JAMES PEALE, do. Gentleman.
JOHN YOUNG, Lower Merrion, Gent.
JOHN STEINMETZ, Philada., do.
ELEAZER LEVY, late of New York, Trader.
JOHN FEGAL, Northern Liberties, Shopkeeper.
JOHN WILLIAMS, Philada., House Carpenter.
19, GEORGE CLAYPOOLE, of Philada., Cabinet Maker.
ANDREW HAMILTON, of do. Gentleman.
EDMOND NUGENT, of do. Breeches maker.
GEORGE FORSYTH, of do. Innholder.
THOMAS HUMPHREYS, Merrion, Philada. Co., Blacksmith.
JAMES CARR, do. Weaver.
LUDWICK KNOLL, do. Farmer.
JACOB BARE, do. do.
JOHN BARE, do. do.
ALEXANDER SOLY, do. Cordwainer.
CHRISTIAN LAWYER, Philada. Co., Labourer.
CONROD GOODMAN, Merrion, Philada. Co., Weaver.
WILLIAM E. GODFREY, Capt. Lieut. Artillery.
DAVID PANCOAST, Philada., House Carpenter.
JOHN MCALESTOR, Yorktown, Commissary.
JOHN FRYHOFFER, Lower Dublin, Phil. Co., Taylor.
WOLLERY FRYHOFFER, do. Farmer.
GEORGE RATZNER, do. do.

1779.
Oct. 19, JOSEPH MATHIAS (his mark), Lower Dublin, Farmer.
    JEREMIAH LYNN, Co. Philada., Shipwright.
    JACOB BAKER, Co. do. Shopkeeper. Affirmed.
    REES PRICE, Philada. County, Farmer. Affirmed.
    WILLIAM DELLAP, Co. Philada., Trader. Affirmed.
    FRANCIS JONES, Philada. County, Gent. Affirmed.
    JOHN LLEWELYN, Lower Merrion, Weaver. do.
    LLEWELYN YOUNG,   do.   Farmer. Affirmed.
    HENRY PUGH,   do.   Weaver. do.
    MORRISS LLEWELYN,   do.   House Carpenter. Affirmed.
    JOSEPH LOWNES, Co. Philada., Silversmith.
    DAVID RIDDLE,   do.   Saddler.
    JOHN DARRACH,   do.   Saddler.
    JOHN BRYAN,   do.   Saddler.
    JOHN CORSE,   do.   do.
    ISAAC PENROSE,   do.   Mercht.
20, JAMES WINTER, of Lower Merrion, Farmer.
    BENJAMIN HOLLAND,   do.   Weaver.
    DAVID ZELL,   do.   Farmer. Affirmed.
    CASPAR WHITEMAN (his mark), do. Farmer.
    JOSEPH BEDFORD, Philada., Gentleman.
    PETER BEDFORD,   do.   do.
    LAWRENCE POWELL, do. Baker.
    WILLIAM TYSON, Blockley, Shoemaker. Affirmed.
    MATTHIAS TYSON, Darby, Farmer. Affirmed.
    WILLIAM MACKENZIE, of Philada., Mercht.
    WILLIAM JEFFERY, Northern Liberties, Labourer.
    JAMES DELAPLAINE, Northern Liberties, Taverner.
    JACOB GOMINGER, Germantown, Miller. Affirmed.

1779.
Oct. 20, STEPHEN BLUNT, Philada., Shoemaker.
 ISAAC LEECH, Cheltenham, Tanner.
 JOHN SPEDE, Philada., Baker.
 EDMOND FAGAN, N. Liberties, Cordwainer.
 MICHAEL MCMULLEN, Lower Merrion, Farmer.
 SAMUEL BAKER, N. Liberties, Ship Carpenter.
 JOSHUA PEARSON, Co. Philada., Cordwainer. Affd.
 WILLIAM FOLLWELL, Philada., Taylor. Affd.
 HUGH KNOX, of Philada. County, Farmer.
 LEONARD KESSLER, of Philada., Joyner.
 ROBERT BELL,   do.   Printer.
 THOMAS CARRADINE, do.   late from Maryland, Mercht.
 GEORGE CLACKNER, of Kingsessing, Taylor.
 JOSEPH LEDRA, of Philada., Bricklayer.
 JOHN LOHRA,   do.   now 18 years of age. Retailer.
 ROBERT CRAIN, made proof that he in March 1778, took the oath to the States before Genl. Green and now before me.
 25, JACOB TREN (his mark), of Passiunk, made oath that he in the year 1777 before Justice Young, took the Oath of Allegiance and the foregoing this day.
Dec. 30, JAMES FARNSWORTH, An inhabitant of Philada. in the year 1777, made Oath that in that year he took the Oath of Allegiance to the States before Justice Smithson in the Jersey State and now before me.

1780.
March 6, JOHN M. JACKSON, now of the age of eighteen years and one month, of Philada., Clark.

(21)

1780.

May 6, PETER OTT, of Blockley Township, Farmer, having taken the test to the States in 1777, was compelled to swear allegiance to the Brittish while here, much against his will as he declares, and which he most heartily renounces.

JOHN DAW, being a Commissioned Officer in the 4th Pensilvania Regt. in the year 1777.

15, DANIEL APPEL, lately from the West Indies, Taylor.

HOSEA SMITH, lately come of age, Taylor.

June 8, JACOB RICKNEAL (his mark), lately discharged from the German American Regt.

JAMES COTTRINGER, of Philada., Brushmaker, but lately arrived to the age of eighteen years.

12, LUKE MORRIS JUNR., Miller, in his minority. Affirmed.

13, WILLIAM DOUGLASS, taken prisoner under age and lately returned.

Note that DANIEL FOLT, of Passiunk not taking the test in time desired now to take it, which he did and I gave a certificate according thereto.

June 28, DANIEL MCLEAN, a Sergeant in the service of this and of the United States the 1st day of June 1778, and since with reputation discharged.

Sep. 9, JAMES KIRK, a soldier in the service of the American United States on the 1st day of June 1778, and since discharged.

25, WILLIAM DUE (his mark), Mariner, resident in this city above five years, being a foreigner unacquainted with the time prescribed by law.

1780.
Sep. 30, MATTHEW PHELPS, of the state of Connecticut, lately from the Mississippi, Planter.
Oct. 10, ISAAC SHELDON, of the State of Connecticut, lately from the Mississippi, Planter.
ABRAHAM HARGIS, a Lieut. in the Continental Army, 10th Pena. Regt. June 1st, 1778.
ROBERT KENNEDY, from South Carolina, Taylor.
21, NICHOLAS HINKLE (his mark), of Blockley, lived in the Jersey State in the year 1776, where he first proved his allegiance.
Dec. 5, PHILIP SWARTZ, charged with treasonable practices and discharged after a long confinement. Recommended by J. C., Sheriff.
13, JOHN ALLEN, of the state of N. Carolina.

1781.
Jan. 29, JOHN COOK (his mark), late of the Jersey state; in Jany. 1779, was qualified to allegiance there before Lemuel Sears in Gloucester County as appears by certificate.
June 14, JOHN JOHNSTON (his mark), by trade a painter and Glazier but has followed the sea some years.
29, JOHN FRAZER (his mark), late a soldier in the Pennsylvania line.
Sep. 7, SAMUEL HEMBEL, formerly a servant in Lancaster co., lately free.
Oct. 8, JAMES HAMPDEN THOMSON, late a citizen of South Carolina and lately arrived in this city from St. Augustine.
9, ADAM GILCHRIST, an officer in the Penna. Line in 1777.

1781.
Oct. 9, GEORGE BOND.
    JOHN PHILE, late a free citizen of Maryland, now of this City, Mercht.
    CHARLES PETTIT.
    JAMES WILLING.
    JAMES MONTGOMERY.
    FRANCIS DONNELLY.
    D. WITHERSPOON.
    WILLIAM HENDERSON.
    WILLIAM GRAHAM, late of Virginia.
  13, BENJ. SMITH (his mark), of Blockley Township, Philada. Co.
Nov. 2, JAMES DUFFY (his mark), now City Constable, Philada.
  21, ANDREW MILLER, of Towamensing, Philada. Co., Farmer.
  20, WILLIAM BELL, of Philada., Taylor, late of the State of New Jersey.

1782.
Feb. 16, THOMAS LAKE, son of Capt. Thomas Lake; now 18 years old.
    JOHN FESMORE (his mark), late discharged from the Penna. Line.
Apl. 15, ELEAZER OSWALD, late Lieut. Col. of Arty. of the United States.
May 1, ARCHIBALD McCLAREY, formerly a private in the river fleet.
  13, BEDFORD WILLIAMS, Surgeon, formerly in the service of the States.
  31, ABRAHAM SEIXAS, formerly an officer in the Militia

1782.

of Charlestown, South Carolina, lately arrived in this city, Mercht.

July 1, WILLIAM BRADFORD, formerly a soldier in the Virginia line, discharged, by trade a Taylor.

13, JOSEPH HELLER, of Merrion Township, lately arrived to the age of 20.

JACOB SIBLEY, of Merrion Township, but lately arrived to the age of 19.

Aug. 7, PHILIP SMITH, a German, bred in Philada., a Taylor by trade.

14, JONATHAN ADAMS, a native of Maryland, by trade a silversmith.

22, MATTHEW BALLAM, a native of New York who retired on the approach of the enemy.

Sep. 14, LEVIN LANGRALL, of the State of Maryland, taken prisoner and escaped from New York, Mariner.

21, ROBERT PATTISON, of Charlestown in South Carolina, Mercht.

Oct. 7, THOMAS STEEL, of Philadelphia, Mariner.

PHILIP MOORE, of Philada., Mercht., having taken the Oath of Allegiance in Boston in 1777 and in the Court of Philada. in April 1782.

JOHN OGDEN, lately arrived to the age of twenty-one years.

JOHN STAFFORD, belonging to the train of Artillery in 1776. Discharged.

JOHN JONES, Health Officer, took the test in Virginia in 1777.

BENJAMIN STAGG, a private in the 5th Penna. Regt. in 1776, discharged in 1781.

1782.
Oct. 7, MICHAEL CONNOR, took the Oath at Reading in June 1778.
DAVID PORTER, an officer in the Penna. Line in 1777.
CHARLES MCCARTER, Surgeon in the 4th Penna. Regt. in 1777.
JAMES MCLEAN, an officer in the Penna. Line in 1777.
LAZARUS STOW, Lieut. in the 11th Penna. Regt. in 1777.
8, JAMES WHITEHEAD.
CHARLES DARRAGH.
MATTHEW MCGUIRE.
WILLIAM GRAY.
ALEXANDER POWER.
JOHN THOMPSON.
JOSEPH RICE.
WILLIAM WILLIAMS.
DAVID ELLIOTT.
PATRICK OWENS, took the test in Virginia in 1777.
JOHN COWELL, surgeon in the Genl. Hospital of Penna. in June 1778.
PATRICK DUFFY, an officer in the Penna. Artillery in 1777.
JOHN KAWORTH, a seafaring man.
JAMES HAMEL, tavern keeper, took the test in Virginia in 1777.
JOHN STRICKER, an officer in the Penna. Line in 1777.
ROBERT SCOT, took the test in Virginia in 1777.

1782.
Oct. 8, JAMES GILCHRIST, an officer in the Penna. Line 1779.
ANDREW LYTLE, an officer in do. 1776.
JOHN BAKER, who took the oath in Virginia, August 1777.
JAMES G. HERRON, late an officer in Hazen's Regiment, Pennsylvania Line.
GEORGE HOFNER, late an officer in the Penna. Line.
JOHN HUNN, took the test in Delaware State 1778.
18, JOHN LOGE, late of Salem, in the State of N. Jersey. Waterman.
Nov. 4, GARRET PETERS, an inhabitant of this City. Shoemaker.
8, ROBERT SMOCK, late of the State of N. Jersey. Clark in the Clothier's Departmt.
19, JOHN BRYARLY, some time resident in this city. Sadler.
WILLIAM PATTON, formerly of Lancaster, in this State. Sadler.
JOHN STILES, some time resident in this city. Sadler.

1783.
Jan. 6, SETH AVERED, from Connecticut, last from Chester Co.
Mch. 19, ANDREW AITKIN, of Philada. Physitian in the Publick service above four years.
April 22, JOHN JAMISON, of Philada. Sadler. Nineteen years of age.
30, GEORGE MAYER, son of Jacob Mayer; a native of Philada., late a prisoner with the enemy, now 19 years old.
May 7, HUGH MARTIN, a surgeon in the Penna. Line in 1778.

1783.
May 30, ADAM STELLER, Butcher, born in Philada., lately of age.
 THOMAS BELL, late apprentice to Geo. Claypoole, Cabinet maker.
June 30, GEORGE TUDOR, a Major in the Penna. Line.
 PHILIP LAUER, having served five years in the Penna. regiment of Artillery.
Sept. 17, JAMES CHRYSTIE, Captain in the Penna. Line.
 JOHN BRICE, formerly Captain in the Marine of this State.
Oct. 6, ABRAHAM HOWELL, of Maurice County, State of New Jersey.
 10, JOSEPH HARMA, Lieut. Col. 1st Regt. of Pennsylvania.
 PHILIP MENTGES, Lieut. Col. in the Southern Army.
 J. MOORE, Major 1st Penna. Regiment.
 JOHN BRYCE, Captain Co. of Artillery.
 13, WILLIAM MARTIN, Captain of Artillery.
 ROBERT WALLACE, proves by certificate that he took the oath of allegiance in the Jersey State in 1777.
 14, EDWARD WHELAN, a soldier in the Penna. line. Discharged.
 ROBERT MORRELL, an artificer in the American Army. Discharged.
 JOHN PATTON, tallow chandler, a native, lately come of age.
 JOHN RHEA, of Philada., a native, lately arrived to age.
 SAMUEL BRADY, Captain 3rd Penna. Regt.

1783.
Oct. 14, THOMAS ADAMS, late of Rhode Island, made oath that he took the test of that State in 1777.

PAUL JONES, Captain in the Navy of the United States.

JOHN SMITH, late Segt. in the Penna. Line. Discharged January 1781.

RICHARD WALLACE (his mark), a private in the Penna. Line. Discharged 1781.

JOHN ADAMS, late a sergeant in the Penna. Line. Discharged Jan. 1781.

THOMAS LAVISYLER, late Ensign in the Penna. Line. Deranged.

ISAAC B. DUNN, Capt. 3rd Regt. Penna.

JAMES FINLEY, makes oath that he in 1777, in Virginia, took the oath of that State of his allegiance.

JOHN HAZLEWOOD, JUNR., lately arrived to the age of 21 years.

CHRISTOPHER KUGLER, of the Northern Liberties, but now arrived to 21 years of age.

L. KEENE, late Captain 2nd Penna. Regt.

EPHRAIM BLAINE, Commissary General Purveyor.

JOHN READ.

ALEXANDER RUSSELL, late Lieut. 7th Penna. Regt.

ALEXANDER BENSTED, late Lieut. & Paymaster 10th Penna. Regt.

THOMAS MCINTIRE.

MARTIN WEYLAND, of Point no Point Northern Liberties, maketh oath which is certified to by Edward Pool, in 1778.

HENRY GREVE, Lieut. in the 4th Penna. Regt.

1784.
Oct. 11, JOHN WHITE, Mate of the General Military Hospital.
    12, ROBERT GREGG, late Captain of the Penna. Line.
        JACOB COX, made oath that he took the oath cɪ allegiance in the Jersey State in 1777.
        JNO. DONOHUE, made oath that he gave test of allegiance in the Jersey State, and since agreeable to law in this State.
        WILLIAM HONEYMAN, formerly a lieut. in the Pensyla. Line.
        WILLIAM NORTON, formerly a private in the Pena. Line. Discharged.
        MATTHEW MCCLENTICK, took the oath in Maryland in 1780.
        PATRICK SHAW (his mark), a private in the Penna. Line. Discharged.

1785.
Feb. 19, ISAAC VAN VLECK, of the Jersey State, appears to have taken the oath of allegiance in that State in 1777.
Apl. 11, EDWARD TILGHMAN, JUNR., of Dover, in the Delaware State, Esq., appears to have taken the oath of allegiance in said State.
Sep. 29, FRANCIS KNOX, Commander of a Vessel under commission in the American Service in the late war.
        JAMES LOCKWOOD, a native of Connecticut, a resident here near two years. Mercht.
Oct. 6, JOHN MITCHELL, of Philada. Mercht.
        JOHN SAVIDGE, a Captain in the Pensilva. Line in 1778.
        PHILIP KLEIN, appears to have taken the oath in

1785.

1778; served in the flying camp, and now before me hath taken the oath.

Oct. 6, JOHN ORGAN (his mark), late a soldier in the Pensyla. Line six years.

JOHN McILENCH (his mark), a soldier in the Pensyla. Line in 1777.

PHILIP COLEWATER (his mark), a soldier in the Pena. Line six years.

24, BARNABY SCULLY, a soldier in the Maryland Line in 1777, since a resident here.

WILLIAM SPOTTSWOOD, from Ireland, resident here about 2 years. Did not take the oath of 1777.

MATTHEW CAREY, from Dublin, Printer, resident here near one year. Did not take the oath of 1777.

1786.

Apl 7, WILLIAM BANKSON, of Philada. Upholsterer, a native of this State, lately arrived to full age.

May 10, ANDREW REY, formerly an officer in the service of the United States, and latterly a resident of the Delaware State.

Oct. 10, DANIEL GARHART (his mark), late a soldier in the American Army, from the commencement of the war.

HENRY LIPSEY, late a soldier in the Artillery of Penna.

HENRY McANALLY, proves that he took the oath in 1778 before Justice Adcock.

JOSEPH CRAWFORD (his mark), proves that he took the test of 1778 in due time.

1786.
Oct. 10, HENRY HARRIS (his mark), proves that he took the oath of 1778 before me in due time.

1787.
Apl. 5, JOSEPH ANDERSON (Esq.), Attorney at Law, formerly a Major in the Army of the United States and the Jersey Line.

13, WILLIAM MONTGOMERY (Esq.), Attorney at Law, formerly a Citizen of the Delaware State.

SECOND BOOK.

We the subscribers do swear (or affirm) that I renounce and refuse all allegiance to George the third, King of Great Britain, his heirs and successors, and that I will be faithful, and bear true allegiance to the commonwealth of Pensylvania as a free and Independant State, and that I will not at any time do or cause to be done any matter or thing that will be prejudicial or injurious to the freedom and Independance thereof, as declared by Congress; and, also, that I will discover and make known to some one Justice of the Peace of this State, all treasons or traitorous conspiracies which I now know or hereafter shall know, to be formed against this or any of the United States of America.

PLUNKETT FLEESON.

Philadelphia, 1778.

1778.
July 11, JAMES HALL.
    JAMES THOMPSON.
    JOHN RIGHTER.
    JOHN KOOK.
  14, JOHANN CHRISTOPHER JUTTER.
    JOHANN CONRAD GOTTHART.
    GEORGE SHARSWOOD.
    JOHN CROOK.
    LUKE KEATING.   2d Certificate proved.
    JOHN PATTERSON.

1778.
July 14, JOHN C. KUNZE.
    15, JOHN HALBURTAT. A 2d Certificate.
        THOMAS HALL. 2d Certificate proved.
        WILLIAM ROBINSON.
        GEORGE CROGHAN.
    20, JOHAN GEORG MILLER.
        ROBERT BASS.
        WILLIAM MATLACK. Affirmed.
        WILLIAM PUGH. Affirmed.
        CHRISTIAN HANSMAN.
        CHRISTOPHER BAKER.
        JOHN BURNES.
        THOMAS BECK. 2d Certificate.
        PASTORIOUS WYNN. 2d Certificate.
    23, WILLIAM JONES.
        CALEB ASH. Affirmed.
        GEORGE STOCKHAM.
    24, ANDREW BRAND. 2d Certificate.
        GEORGE BATES. do.
        ADAM CLAMPFFER. do.
        JACOB FISLER.
    25, JACOB CARRICK (his mark).
        JACOB CONROD (his mark).
        JACOB LATCH (his mark).
        SAMUEL TOM (his mark).
        GEORGE KURTZ, sworn to have taken the oath of
            allegiance the 30th June 1777. 2d Certificate.
        FRANCIS FINLEY. 2d Certificate.
        GEORGE FOX.
    27, NN. SELLERS.

1778.
July 27, FRIEDERICH PLACK, swore that he took the test and had a certificate from me in June 1777. 2d Certificate.
JAMES NEILL. Affirmed.
WILLIAM BARNS.
JOHN CUMMINGS.
CONRAD DEWETTER, attests having taken the oath and had my certificate the 26th day of June 1777.
28, JOHN BROWN, Cabinet maker, testifies that on or about the latter end of June 1777, he took the oath, and had my certificate. 2nd Certificate.
WILLIAM MOORE.
JOHN SMITH, of Philada. Breeches maker, sworn, that about the end of June 1777, he took the oath of allegiance, and had a certificate from me, which he hath lost, and now has a 2nd certificate.
29, REES PRICE. Affirmed.
30, WILLIAM STROUD. Affirmed.
JOHN COFFMAN.
GEORGE WOOD.
MATTHIAS NONVELLER, of Blockly, attests to having in June 1777, taken the test, and had my certificate, which he hath lost. 2d Certificate.
JACOB BEALERT, of Blockly, attests to having in June 1777, or thereabout, taken the oath of allegiance, and that he had my certificate, which he hath lost. 2d Certificate.
THOMAS WATTS.
31, GEORGE CHANDLER.

1778.
July 31, Elijah Coffin.   2d Certificate.
  James Harris.
  Richard Price.   Affirmed.
Aug. 1, Thomas Irwin.
  W. Hamilton.
  Jacob Ash, Attests having taken the test with me about June 1777.   2nd Certificate.
  Philip Conrad, Attests to have taken the test about July, 1777.
  Martin Walter.
  William McElvain.
 3, Peter Crass (his mark), Attests to have taken the test in or about the Month of July 1777.
  Jonathan Draper.
  John Corman.
  Edward Richie.
  Rudolph Sibley (his mark).
  William Whittington, of Boston.
  John Overly, Copy from ye Original Sept. 12th 1777.   No. 887.
  Richard Hunt, Attests to have taken the Test of me in July 1777, & now has a 2d Certificate.
 4, Gunning Bedford.
  George Claypoole.
  John Keichler (his mark).
  Isaac Widdos, Attests to have taken the Oath & to have lost his Certificate taken in June 1777.   2d Certificate.
  John Weaver.
  Charles Cecil, lately arrived from Europe.

1778.
Aug. 4, JOHN DAVIS. Affirmed.
 5, ISAAC WARNER, did take the test in 1777; was constrained to swear allegiance to the King, which he now doth renounce. 2d Certificate.
 ARCHIBALD MCKENDRICK, a Brittish officer, discharged from parole, and recommended.
 LUDWICK KNOLL.
 CONROD GOODMAN. Affirmed.
 DARBY SAVAGE.
 RICHARD TOPLIFF, Copy from Original June 13 1777. No. 32.
 6, JAMES SPINKS.
 FRIEDERICH DESHONG, took the oath to the States in 1777, was after constrained to swear allegiance to the crown, which he now renounces, and again takes the test to the States. 2d Certificate.
 JACOB LITCHENHAM (his mark).
 BENJAMIN THAW.
 7, LUDWIG FALKENSTEIN.
 PETER REMENDER (his mark).
 SAMUEL EVANS. Affirmed.
 SAMUEL LANGDALE.
 ARCHIBALD WATSON (his mark).
 8, JAMES DAVIS.
 WILLIAM SAUNDERS, Attests to have Attested in July 1777. 2nd Certificate.
 HUGH ROSS, Attests to have taken & subscribed in July 1777. 2d Certificate.
 10, JOHN DIAMOND.
 JACOB ERRINGER.

1778.
Aug. 10, JOHANNES HELLER.
CHARLES STOW.
CHRISTOPHER HART (his mark), took the test from me in June 1777, per qualification. 2nd Certificate.
EDWARD McDONNELL.
JOSEPH GOVETT.
JAMES PACKER. Affirmed.
JOHN ALLEN (his mark), gunsmith. 2nd Certificate.
JOHN YERGER.
JOSEPH WILLIAMSON.
11, THOMAS FLEESON, A 2nd certificate 17th July, 1777.
MELCHOIR NUFF, taken in Augt. 1777. 2d Certificate.
SAMUEL STERN.
12, THEOBALD ENT, Sadler, Attested taking in June 1777. 2d Certificate.
ADAM GROFF (his mark).
JAMES RUSSELL.
JOHN HEYL, Attests to having taken the Oath in June 1777. 2nd Certificate.
PHILIP WARNER, known to have taken the oath in June 1777. 2d Certificate.
BENJAMIN HUMPHREYS. Affirmed.
JOSEPH LEONARD. Affirmed.
13, JOHN DAVID.
RICHARD ROBINSON, who farther attests to have taken the Oath before George Brian, Esq., about the month of July 1777, but lost his Certificate. 2d Cert.

1778.
Aug. 14, WILLIAM SOWERSBY.
 WILLIAM LAKE, renewed his Certificate 27th Augt. 1777. No. 850. 2nd Certificate.
 GEORGE CONNELL, Carver, renewed his Certificate of 28th June 1777. No. 194. 2d Cert.
 DAVID RICHARDS, Affirms to have taken the test on or about July 1777. Renewed his Certificate.
 WILLIAM GUINEY.
 JACOB BAKER.
15, EDWARD CAVANAUGH (his mark).
 WILLIAM ROBINSON.
 JACOB HANKEL, Took the test before me about Augt. 1777.
 CORNELIUS BARNES.
 PETER MELLEN.
 THOMAS ROUE.
17, WILLIAM THOMSON.
 THOMAS PALMER.
 JOSEPH LISLE.
 –ROBERT DAVIDSON, Took the test in the Delaware State the 2d of June 1778.
 JACOB KINNARD.
 JACOB BURKLAE.
18, JAMES RASBOTHAM.
 ROBERT MOORE, Proves having taken the test of John Crugh, Esq., of Carlisle, which he hath lost. Now taken of me. 2d Certificate.
 JOHN REILEY JUNR., Attests to have in 1777 taken test to the States, in Maryland, and lost his certificate.

F

1778.
Aug. 18, GEORGE YOUNG.
  ROBERT BELL. 2d Certificate.
  JOHANNES HILARIUS BAKER.
 19, JAMES UNDERWOOD, Affirms to having taken the test & had my certificate in or about Augt. 1777.
  PHILIP YOUNG (his mark).
  RICHARD SINGELTON.
  SIMON HUFTY.
  JOHN COTTMAN.
  THOMAS MORGAN. Affirmed.
  WILLIAM CLARK. Affirmed.
 20, GERARD WILLIAM BEEKMAN, 2d Certificate & abjurations.
  THOMAS THOMPSON.
  WILLIAM GRAHAM, known to have taken the test in June 1777, No. 92, Copy.
 21, ROBERT PLUNKET.
  JOHN ARMITAGE, took the test in July 1777. 2d Certificate.
 22, JACOB BARR.
  JOHN LEAR (his mark).
  JOHN ROBERTS. Affirmed.
  SAMUEL JUNKIN.
  NICHOLAS RICE.
  GEORGE MATZINGER.
  EVAN GRIFFITH.
  FRANCIS JONES. Affirmed.
  CHRISTIAN WORTZHEISER.
  GABRIEL KORN, proves to have taken in July 1777.

1778.
Aug. 24, JOHN LONG, proves having taken the Oath in July 1777.
  MATTHEW FOY, proves to have taken of me about July 1777.
  WILLIAM KEMBLE.
  WILLIAM MOORE.
  WILLIAM DOMILLER (his mark).
25, JOHN GRAVEL, proves to have taken the Oath in July 1777.
  JAMES DEXTER, proves to have taken the Oath in June 1777. 2d Certificate.
  GEORGE LORDEN, proves to have taken the Oath in July, 1777.
26, WILLIAM BEALE.
  WILLIAM TUSTIN.
  WILLIAM TREMPOR, proves having taken the Oath in or about July, 1777.
  DANIEL HARAR.
  JOSEPH SELLERS. Affirmed.
  ADAM METTS, proves having taken the Oath in Augt. 1777.
  JOHN FORD, proves having taken the Oath in July 1777.
  WILHELM BASTIAN.
  THOMAS FITZGERALD, proves that he took the Oath on 30th of June 1777.
  THOMAS FRANCIS, at the same time, and now has his first Certificate. No. 426.
  JOHN VANNOST.

1778.
Aug. 27, CHRISTOPHER REID, swore that he took the test in June 1777.
JOHN HENDERSON.
THOMAS PASCHALL.
JOSEPH HILLBORN.

We the Subscribers do swear (or affirm) that I renounce and refuse all allegiance to George the Third, King of Great Britain, his heirs and successors, and that I will be faithful and bear true allegiance to the Commonwealth of Pensylvania as a free and Independent State; and that I will not at any time do or cause to be done, any matter or thing, that will be prejudicial or injurious to the freedom and Independence thereof, as declared by Congress; and, also, that I will discover and make known to some one Justice of the Peace of the said state all treasons or traitorous conspiracies which I now know or hereafter shall know to be formed against this or any of the United States of America.

PLUNKET FLEESON.

Philadelphia, 1778.

1778.
Aug. 27, JOHN LENNERD, Weaver.
    28, JOHN THOMAS, Also proves to have taken the Oath from Justice Davis, of Chester Co., in 1777.
    MICHAEL DITRICH.
    JACOB RENNO, proves to have taken the Oath in July, 1777.
    JOSEPH PARKES, proves to have taken the Oath in Augt. 1777.
    JOHN BROOKES, proves that he had taken the Oath June 28th 1777.

1778.

Aug. 28, JOHN PALMER, proves to have taken the Oath in June 1777.

THOMAS CRAIG, proves to have taken the Oath on or about Augt. 1777.

STEPHEN SIMONS, proves to have taken the Oath in Jany. 1777.

WILLIAM PINTON, proves taking the Oath in June 1777.

29, JACOB WHITMAN.

FELIX BENTLEY.

GEORGE KOOPER (his mark), proves that he took the test in 1777, & now before me renounces the allegiance extorted by the Brittish.

WILLIAM MCMICHAEL, proves taking the test in July, 1777.

CONRAD STOLTZ, renounces the Allegiance sworn to the Brittish, and taken by force last winter.

CHRISTOPHER MILLER, renounces as above.

EDMOND NUGENT.

31, EDMOND BEECH JUNR., Copy of original July 1st 1777.

JOHN MARTIN, proves to have taken the test in Augt. 1777.

JOSEPH PEMBERTON.

HOYMON LUY, proves that he did take the test in Augt. 1777.

JAMES OELLERS, proves that in June 1777 he did take the test, but was constrained to Brittish Allegiance, and this day renews his Allegiance to the State.

1778.
Sept. 2, ABRAHAM GLOEDING, proves to have taken the test in June 1777.
CHRISTIAN PETERMAN.
GEORGE MAKEMSON.
3, HENRY CRESS, proves to have taken the test to the United States in 1777; was constrained to Brittish Allegiance, and this day renounces the latter & swears allegiance to the United States.
FRANCIS BOWER, swears to have taken the test in 1777 before Justice Hull, of Connecocheque, and now before me.
COOPER BRETHOWER, proves to have taken the test in Augt. 1777.
4, MICHAEL CLARK, sworn to have taken the test to the State in July 1777.
ENNION WILLIAMS, proves to have taken the test of me in June, 1777.
JONATHAN HEATON.
5, ANTHONY KIRK (his mark).
CASPER SOUDER, took the test in June 1777; has since been constrained to swear allegiance to the Brittish, and this day renews his first oath.
7, THOMAS RENSHAW, proves to have taken the State test in June, 1777. No. 17. 2nd Certificate. Affirmed.
JOHN TOMKINS.
JOHN EVERLY (his mark).
8, WILLIAM DAVIDSON, a prisoner and on parole, from the 16th of November to this time.
BARTHOLOMEW THAYER.

1778.
Sept. 8, JOSEPH HIBBERD.
    SAMUEL PENROSE.
   9, THOMAS WELCH. Affirmed.
    JOSEPH HONEYCOMB, proves to have taken the State test in 1777.
    MATTHEW HOOPER, proves to have taken the State test in June 1777.
    JOHN COATES, proves that he took the State test in June 1777.
    JOSEPH BOLTER, proves that he took the State test in June 1777.
    IMANUEL JACOB ALBORN.
  11, JAMES MURDAUGH.
    EDWARD FLOUNDERS, proves to have taken the test of me in August 1777. Affirmed.
  12, BENJAMIN MILLER.
    THOMAS ROSSITER JUNR.
    JOHN ARMET, proves to have taken the test of me in June, 1777.
  14, MATHIAS COPE, proves that he took of me the test in July 1777.
    JOHN GREBLE, of Philadelphia, Cooper, before Justice Young, in June 1777, took the test, since which he was constrained to swear allegiance to the Brittish, and now renews his former test.
  15, ANDREW HAMILTON.
    JACOB ZINCK, of Moyamensing, took the test of Benjamin Paschal in June 1777; was constrained to that of the Brittish, and now before me renounces the latter.

1778.

Sept. 17, BENJAMIN TOTTIE, proves that he in June 1777, took the test to the State before me. 2nd Certificate.

DAVID SALDRICH (his mark), not 18 years of age the 1st of June last.

18, PETER GRAB.

WILLIAM STOLL.

19, JAMES WEST.

JEROM INGIEZ, proves to have taken the State test in June 1777.

JOHN MATHES.

21, JOSEPH PALMER, proves his Attestation in June, 1777, before me.

24, TOBIAS RUDOLPH, proves his Attestation in Augt. 1777.

JACOB EHRENZELLER, proves his Attestation in June 1777.

25, CHRISTIAN RUDOLPH.

JAMES WALSH, proves his Attestation in June 1777.

26, SOLOMON HALLING, Second Surgeon in the General Military Hospitals.

THOMAS McDOWELL.

JOSEPH WOOD.

28, GEORGE HEYL, took the test of me the 25th day of June 1777; was constrained to swear allegiance to the Brittish, which he hath this day renounced.

WILLIAM ECKHART.

JOHN ORD ESQ., took the test July 10th 1777, & was constrained to swear allegiance to the Brittish, which he this day hath renounced.

1778.
Sept. 28, CHARLES PHILE, 1st Lt.
JACOB LEHRÉ, proves to have Attested in June 1777.
ROBERT FULLERTON.
29, ANDREW GEORGE (his mark).
JAMES KINKEAD proves to have attested in Augt. 1777.
Oct. 2, WILLIAM MCCLATCHIE, proves to have attested before me in August 1777.
CHARLES STEWART.
3, DANIEL GOSNER, proves to have attested in June 1777.
JARED SAXTON.
JOHN PORTER, late of Philada., proves to have taken the State test in June 1777. Affirmed. 2nd Certificate.
JUSTINIAN FOX, proves to have taken the State test of me in June 1777. 2nd Certificate.
5, JAMES KELLEY, proves that at Carlisle, in February last, he took the Oath of Allegiance.
6, JOHN HELM, 1st Lieut. of 6th Penna. Regt., late a prisoner.
JOHN GEORGE (his mark), Schuylkill.
JOHN GEORGE JUNR. (his mark), Blockley.
CHRISTIAN DISHONG.
9, EDMOND TOBIN.
JOHN WHITE, proves to have taken the State test before me in June 1777.
10, DAVID SELLERS.
CHRISTOPHER MIERS (his mark).

(51)

1778.
Oct. 12, JOHN LAWRENCE, Lieut., late prisoner of War.
    JOHN MORGAN, Lieut.,   do.   do.
    GEORGE GEORGE, proves to have taken the State test in Augt. 1777, before me.
    CHARLES GREER, a prisoner with the Enemy, while in the City.
    CHRISTIAN SLEIGH (his mark), proves to have taken the State Test in Augt. 1777.
    JOHN KERLIN JUNR., proves to have taken the State test in Augt. 1777.
    BENJAMIN SCULL, took the State test before me, the 2d day of Sept. 1777. No. 862.
    JOHN MCKENNAN.
    JOHN STUART.
14, WILLIAM GLISSON.
    JOHN KOEHMLE, proves that he in June 1777, did take the Legal test before me.
    JOHN CALBANAN, proves that he was Qualified, before me, in June 1777.
    JOHN CLAZER (his mark), proves that he was Qualified before me in Sept. 1777.
    MICHAEL GITTS, proves that he was qualified before me in June 1777.
15, THOMAS BOOKER, proves that he was qualified in June 1777.
    PHILIP HOFFER,   do.   do.
    MATTHIAS WEISS,   do.   do.
16, THOMAS WADE (his mark).
    MICHAEL CANER, proves that he was qualified in July 1777, swore allegiance to the Brittish, and now renounces the same.

1778.
Oct. 17, THOMAS DICKSON, Cutter, renewed his certificate, 27th Augt. 1777. No. 849.
 JOHN CROOK, proves that he was qualified in June 1777.
 19, CHRISTIAN DAME, proves to have taken the test June 30th 1777.
 JOHN FORSTER (his mark), Farmer.
 C. MARTIN FORSTER (his mark).
 ROBERT ROBSON (his mark), Mariner, a Brittish Prisoner.
 DAVID TAGGART.
 20, WILLIAM ARMSTRONG, of Philadelphia County, Major. Copy from Original June 30, 1777. No. 327.
 21, JOHN RIDDLE, State Officer. Copy from Original June 30, 1777.
 25, JOHN HIGNET KEELING.
 JOHN CAMPBELL, proves taking the test in July 1777.
Nov. 2, WILLIAM WILSON.
 CHARLES RITTER, proves to have taken the Oath before me in June 1777, was constrained to swear allegiance to the Brittish, which he hath now renounced.
 ANDREW DOZ, late an Inhabitant of Jersey, where he took the Oath, as required by the law of that state.
 MICHAEL GRATZ, late residing in Virginia, where he took the Oath to that state.
 HEINRICH KIMMEL.

1778.
Nov. 7, JACOB MAUR, proves to have taken the test in June 1777.
    WILLIAM STANLEY, schoolmaster, took the test in June 1777.
  9, SHEWBART ARMITAGE.
  10, PETER DE HAVEN, of Philada., Gentleman, produces his Certificate taken of me, 26th June 1777.
  13, ISAAC HAYES, Blockley.
  14, MICHAEL SCHMYSER, a prisoner lately exchanged.
  16, SAMUEL HUMPHREYS, took the test in 1777.
  17, JOHANN GEORGE DEGENHART, a Hessian Deserter.
  18, RICHARD LUDGATE (his mark).
  19, ALEXANDER TOD, took the Oath before me, June 1777.
  25, JOHN STONEMAN, Bensalem, took the test in 1777, of Col. Kirkbride. Sworn.
  26, FREDERICK LINT, took the Oath in June 1777, was constrained to Brittish Allegiance, which he now hath renounced & renewed the former.
    BENJAMIN CHAPMAN JUNR. Affirmed.
    FRIEDERICH ERMANBERGER.
    MARTIN PIERIE.
  27, GEORGE STOUTE, Northern Liberties, took the test in June 1777.
    JOHN LINNIBERGER (his mark).
    HEINRICH KATZ, Whitemarsh.
  28, GEORGE PEISS, Passiunk.
    GODFREY SHISLER, do.
    JOHN WHITE, do.

(54)

1778.

Nov. 30, MICHAEL SHIVER (his mark), proves to have taken the test of me, in June 1777.

GEORGE SHAW, proves to have taken the test of me in 1777.

Dec. 2, WILLIAM GUINOP, proves to have taken the test before me in 1777.

4, SAMUEL COUTTY, swears to have taken the test before me in the year 1777.

5, FELIX LIBERSTIN.

CASPER CLEIGNER (his mark).

NICHOLAS QUEST (his mark).

7, FREDERICK DUY.

JOHN HIFFERNAN.

JOHN WHITEMAN (his mark), late of Northern Liberties, Philada. County, proves by evidence, to have taken the Oath June 13th 1777.

MORRIS WORREL, proves to have taken the Oath in June 1777.

10, GEORG GEBHEART, swears to have taken the test in June 1777.

JOSEPH LEWIS, on oath did take the test before me in July 1777.

WILLIAM NICHOLAS (his mark), did take the test in June 1777.

SAMUEL CRISPIN, on oath did take the test on or about June 1777.

WILLIAM ASHTON, on oath did take the test on or about June 1777.

JOHN FRALEY, on oath did take the test on or about June 1777.

According to the Act of 5th Decr. 1778.

1778.
Dec. 11, HEINRICH SCHWALLACH.
    PETER POWELL, on oath did take the test on or about June 1777, before me.
    EDWARD RIFFETS, on oath did take the test in June 1777 before me.
18, MATHEW KNOX, Lieut., on oath proves that he was taken prisoner at fort Washington, exchanged the 22d September last, and returned to this State, the 24th of last month.
    WILLIAM CLARK, on Oath proves that he did take the Oath before me in 1777.
    DONALD McINTOSH, foreigner, lately in the Brittish Service.
    JOHN EVERHART, on oath proves that in June 1777, he testified Allegiance before me.

1779.
Jan. 1, JOHANNES MÜLLER, a foreigner lately in the Brittish army.
5, JOHN LINTON, in June 1777 did take the test before me.
    GEORGE SNYDER, on oath did take the Affirmation in 1777.
8, PHILIP HEINRICHS, a foreigner lately in the Brittish service.
11, ABRAHAM WAYNE, on oath proves that he did take & subscribe the test in 1777.
22, DAVID EVERHARD, on oath proves that he did take and subscribe the test in June 1777.

1779.
Jan. 25, SAMUEL CHANNELL, on oath proves that he did take the test before me in June 1777.

27, ANDREW DAY, on oath proves that he did take the test oath before me in August 1777.

JEREMIAH WILLIAMS, on oath proves that he did take the test before me, in 1777.

Feb. 13, JACOB STETTENFIELD, a foreigner lately in the Brittish service.

CHRISTIAN OVERSTAKE (his mark), Northern Liberties, proves to have taken the test before me in 1777.

23, JAMES LIGHT, did take and subscribe the oath of allegiance before me the 3rd day of September 1777. Copy from Original.

25, JOHN MITCHEL, did take and subscribe the oath as by law directed in June 1777. 2d Certificate.

ANDREW ZEIGLER, of Swedesford did take the affirmation in June 1777.

March 16, JOHN FISHER, proves that he did take the test before me in 1777.

19, JOHN BARNHILL JUNR., not until now of the age of 18 years.

DAVID BEALER proves that he did take the test in the year 1777.

Apl. 2, WILLIAM LAWRENCE, on oath proves that he did take and subscribe as by law directed in 1777.

6, BENJAMIN MCVEAGH, by oath proves that he did take & subscribe as by law directed in 1777.

JOHN JACOB TRANSO, a German. A deserter from the Brittish.

1779.
Apl. 6, RICHARD TAYLOR, lately from Britain.
May 11, CHARLES BITTERS of Philada. late Breeches maker, made oath that he did take & subscribe before me in or about July 1777.
    PHILIP STOCK, Gardner, on oath proves that he did take the test before me in June 1777.
17, THOMAS RICHMAN formerly a soldier in the Brittish Army. Deserted April 11, 1778.
    GEORGE STOKES, on oath proves that he did take & subscribe in June 1777.
    WILLIAM FECUNDAS, on Oath proves that he took & subscribed the oath in June 1777.
19, JEREMIAH QUIN, on Oath proves that he took & subscribed the Oath of Allegiance in June 1777.
20, MICHAEL GAMEBER, of Philada., Cooper, proves that he did take the test 27th June, 1777.
21, JOHANNES POTH, proves that he took the Oath required by law, the 22d day of July 1777.
    ADAM POTH JUNR., proves that he took the Oath of Allegiance required, on the 22d day of July 1777.
    WILLIAM HUNT, on Oath proves that about August in the year 1777, he did take & subscribe the oath according to law.
22, FRANTZ WILHELM HETTMANNKERGER, by evidence proves that he took & subscribed in July 1777.
    JOHN HAIN, proves by evidence his taking before me in July 1777.
24, WILLIAM BROWN, of Philada., Tavern-Keeper, did in June 1777, take the test as appears by his Certificate. No. 447.

(58)

1779.

May 26, RICHARD SKELLORN, of Phila., Brass Founder, proves that he in 1777, before me took the Oath.

28, DANIEL SPENCER, proves that he in July 1777, did then take the test.

WILLIAM GOGGIN, Mariner, lately in the Brittish Service.

June 16, CORNELIUS COMEGYS JUNR., of Maryland, proves taking the test, according to law, in the year 1777.

JACOB BARGE, did affirm to the allegiance, according to law, in the year 1777.

17, ADAM LECHLER, proves that he did take the test, as by law directed in June 1777.

21, WILLIAM ALEXANDER, Son of Alexr. Alexander of this City, impressed by the Brittish in 1776, and in their service until June 1778.

26, WILLIAM WESTON, by evidence proves having taken the test in 1777.

July 30, PETER BAYNTON, testifies that he did take the test of Allegiance in 1777.

JAMES ROGERS, testifies that he took the test before me in 1777.

31, CASPER GOSNER, proves by Philip Wenemon his having taken the test before me in 1777.

CHRISTOPHER REED, proves by Capt. John Peters, that he took the test in the year 1777.

FRANCIS GUSSE, of Philada., Goldsmith, as appears by his certificate took the Oath of Allegiance, ye 28th day of June 1777. Was sworn by the Brittish.

1779.
July 31, GEORG BARDEEK, of Philada., Silversmith, proves by Francis Gusse, that he took the test ye 28th day of June 1777.

ROBERT FULLERTON, of Philada., Painter, proves by Capt. Joseph Wathens that he did take the test in the year 1777.

JOSEPH BOULTER, of Philada., Shoemaker, by Cadr. Dickinson, proves having taken the test before me in 1777.

CONRAD HANS, of Philada., Coachmaker, testifies having taken the test in the year 1777.

Aug. 2, CHRISTOPHER ADAMS, testifies that he took the test before me in the year 1777.

JOHN POLLARD, testifies that he did take the test before me, in the year 1777.

JOHN NICE, proves by Samuel Shrive that he took the test before Henry Chrest of Reading, the 21st day May 1778.

ALLAN MCCOLLIN, proves that he did take the test by Affirmation before me in the year 1777.

SAMUEL HONEYMAN, proves that he took the test in the year 1777.

JOSEPH ROBINETT, proves to have taken the test in 1777.

4, PETER GRANT, now of Philada., proves by Conrad Swetzer, that he in the year 1777 before Joshua Elder of Lancaster, did take the Oath of Allegiance.

JOHN ADAM KOEHLER, a deserter from the Brittish Army, now of Philada. Pewterer.

1779.

Aug. 4, GEORGE REINHART, proves to have taken the test, before me in the year 1777.

THOMAS DEAK, proves to have taken the test in 1777, before me.

8, JOHN HETHERINGTON, proves by Ludwick Shuder, that he took the test before Justice Moore, in the year 1777.

CHARLES LORDEN, of Philada., proves that he did take the test before me in 1777.

GEORGE HARLY, of Philada., Taylor, proves by Alexander Greenwood, that he took the test before me in the year 1777.

ALEXANDER GREENWOOD (his mark), of Philada., Shoemaker, proves by George Harley, that he took the test before me in the year 1777.

12, CONRAD ECKELMAN, proves by John Smith, that he, before me, in the year 1777, took the Oath.

BENEDICT SNEIDER, proves that he took the test before me in 1777.

JOHN SUTTON, proves that he took the test before me in the year 1777.

15, ALBRIGHT HAZLETON, proves that he took the test before me in the year 1777.

CASPER STULL, proves by Joseph Wathings that he took the test before me, in the year 1777.

ANDREW YOUNG, proves by certificate that he took the test with me in June 1777.

MATTIS POT, proves by Coron Kephard that he took the test before me in June 1777.

ABRAHAM ROBERTS, proves by Certificate that he took the test before me in June 1777. No. 476.

1779.
Aug. 15, CONRAD SCHIN, proves that he did take the test before me in the year 1777.

    STEPHEN FOURAGE, proves that he took the test before me in 1777.

    GEORGE RUTTER, proves that he took the test before me in the year 1777.

    DANIEL CRAIG, of Philada., Hatter, proves that he took the test before me in the year 1777.

    MICHAEL KRAFST, Tanner, proves by David Reshong that he did take the test before me in June 1777.

    DAVID RESHONG, of Philada., Taylor, produces Certificate that he did take the test before me, June 30th 1777. No. 404.

    JOSEPH OGDEN JUNR., proves that he took the test, the 1st day of July 1777, by Certificate produced.

    EDWARD HUSTON, by Joseph Ogden Junr., proves that he took the Oath, the 1st day of July 1777.

19, CHARLES BLATZER. See the other record.

We the Subscribers do swear (or affirm) that I do renounce & refuse all allegiance to George the Third King of Great Britain, his heirs and successors; and that I will be faithful and bear true Allegiance to the Commonwealth of Pensilvania, as a free and Independent State; and that I will not at any time do or cause to be done any matter or thing that will be prejudicial or injurious to the freedom & Independence thereof as declared by Congress; and also that I will discover and make known to some one Justice of the said State, all treasons & traitorous conspiracies, which I now know, or hereafter shall know to be formed against this or any of the United States of America.

PLUNKET FLEESON.

Philadelphia, 1779.

1779.
- Aug. 14, LEWIS NICE, State Officer, proves that he in June 1777, before me did take the Oath of Allegiance as by law directed.
- 21, JACOB SMITH, late of this City, Harness-Maker, proves by James Gilingham, that he before me, in the year 1777, took the Oath of Allegiance as by law directed.
- 27, JOSHUA BURN, of Philada., Potter, proves by Original Certificate that the 1st day of July 1777, before me took the test of Allegiance according to Law. Original Certificate produced.

1779.

Sept. 1, CHRISTOPHER BURLY, proves that he in the Year 1777, before me took the Oath of Allegiance as by law directed.

ISRAEL MATTSON, of Philada., proves by James Lyons, that he before me did take the Oath as by law directed, in the year 1777.

2, ANDREW PARKHILL, proves by Daniel McCarey that he before me, took the Oath as by law directed, 30th June 1777.

DANIEL MCCARY, of Philada., by Original Certificate proves that he took the Oath as by law directed before me the 30th June 1777.

27, THOMAS MESNARD, late a Brittish subject & lately from New-York.

30, JONATHAN STANTON, late in the Brittish service, now residing in this City. Breeches-Maker.

Oct. 11, JAMES GAMBLE, lately in the Brittish Sea service, as a Mariner.

WILLIAM VAUGHAN HITCHINGS, in the Brittish Mercht. Service, lately taken by an American Privateer.

12, DANIEL BARNHILL, lately returned from the Brittish fleet, into which he was pressed.

JOSEPH RUE, made proof that he took the test, the 1st day of July 1777. No. 665.

JACOB SCHRACK, proves by Edward Neffetts, that he took the test before me in June 1777.

THOMAS CHANNELL, took & subscribed the test before me, the 26th day of June 1777 as per Original Certificate.

1779.
Oct. 12, JOHAN CONRAD BECKMAN, late a soldier in the Hessian Army.

13, JACOB BOWER, late of Moyamensing, by testimony of Rudolph Feel, took and subscribed the Oath of Allegiance in June 1779.

14, SAMUEL SMITH, on affirmation proves that he took & subscribed the test of Allegiance in the year 1777.

20, JOSEPH BULKELEY, Mercht., lately arrived in this State from the Island of Eustatia.

WILLIAM SHIELL, M.D., lately arrived in this City from the City of Dublin.

Dec. 10, JOHAN PETER AHL, Taylor, a Hessian late in the Brittish Service.

CASPER LOVING, Taylor, a Hessian late in the Brittish Service.

PIERRE LEMAIGRE, a subject of France lately from that Kingdom, via N. York.

NICHOLAS PERREE, a native of France, lately from Guadelope.

22, JOHANN PANRERT, a Hessian late in the Brittish Service.

YORICK WUSMAN, a Hessian late in the Brittish Service.

27, JOSEPH OGDEN JUNR., proves by Original Certificate that he took & subscribed the test on affirmation, the 1st day of July 1777.

29, JOHANN XHART MELLOR, Baker, a Hessian from N. York, late in the Brittish service.

1780.
Jan. 4, JAMES LINCOLN, late from the City of Dublin.

1780.
Jan. 12, WILLIAM PRICHARD, lately from the Island of St. Eustatia.

Feb. 7, GEORGE MOORE, lately from the Massachusetts State where he took the Oath to the United States.

12, KERENCE DOWLING (his mark), late in the Hessian Army, deserted at the Battle of Monmouth, since a residenter in this State, by trade a woolcomber, & well recommended to me.

March 2, JAMES NUGENT, formerly a resident in the Jersey State, now of Philada.

April 8, JOHN SNELHART (his mark), a Hessian Deserter from the Brittish at N. York.

24, JOHN L. LEAR, Baker, a Hessian deserter from New York. Entered the American Service.

May 13, WILLIAM LINNARD, made Oath that he took the Oath of Allegiance, according to Law, in the month of June 1777, and hath lately lost his Certificate.

MARTIN CHRIST (his mark), deserted the Brittish Army, being an Anspacher & since the Army left this City.

16, PATRICK REILEY, Shoemaker, who says that he deserted the Brittish Service in 1778 & swore Allegiance to the States in that year, at Pitts Grove in this State & has lost his Certificate.

18, JOHN CONNOR, lately arrived from the Kingdom of Ireland. Mercht.

SIMÉON MEYLAND, a native of Switzerland, some time a resident in this City; by trade a Lapidary or Jeweller.

1780.
June 3, CARL LUDEWIG BARON V. BILOW, a Hessian, some time in the Brittish Service.

CHRISTIAN VON BECK, a Hessian, some time in the Brittish Service.

10, PHILIP BOUTMAN (his mark), of Southwark, by Thomas Booker proves that he took the test before in the year 1777.

WILLIAM PERKINS, late a Volunteer in Col. Mayland's Dragoons proves that he took the test about the month of Sept. in the year 1777. No. 900.

FRANCIS COLSON, House Carpenter, now a trader; lately arrived in this State from Hispaniola.

GEORG JOHNER, a Hessian, deserted from the Brittish Service in 1778.

12, ADAM SHETZLINE (his mark), has made proof by Godfred Gebler, that he took the test 29th June 1777.

GEORGE SPEEL, of Passiunk Township, made proof that he took the test before me in 1777.

CHRISTIAN LUTS, proves by John Young of Passiunk, that he did take the test in the year 1777.

DANIEL BARNS, of Philada., bricklayer proves from Original, that he took the test 1st day of July 1777.

DAVID NAER, of Philada., Nailor, proves by Godfrey Wetzel that he took the test 30th June, 1777.

14, JOHN HUGHES, Practitioner in Physick, lately arrived in this City from Hispaniola.

15, THOMAS SIMMONS, proves by Philip Boatman, that he took the test before me in 1777.

1780.
June 15, WILLIAM GRAY, of Philada., Brewer, proves by Original Certificate that he affirmed to the State test, the 26th June 1777.
    27, THOMAS SMITH, a native of Bermuda, just arrived in this port from thence.
    28, JAMES ALENBY, of Philada., Cooper proves by Rowland Pritchett, that he took the test before me in or about July 1777.
        ROWLAND PRITCHETT, of Philada., Cooper, produces his Original Certificate No. 202 dated 28th June 1777.
    30, WILLIAM BARBER, Captain, late a prisoner in Hispaniola; admitted to take the Oath of Allegiance (by order of Council).
July 11, JOHANNES SCHMITT, a Hessian, deserted from the Brittish in the year 1778, now married & settled in Springfield, Philada. Co.
    20, JOHAN BARNARD SIMON, a Hessian, deserted from the Brittish army at New York, by trade a taylor, now married & settled in this City.
    28, GEORGE KNOEPLER, a High German, deserted from the Brittish October 1779; recommended by John Jervis.
        JOHN TELMAN, a German, deserted from the Brittish in October 1779, with a pass from the American Camp.
    31, CHARLES TEIGH, a Hessian deserted from the Brittish in 1779, a hair dresser, married & settled in this City; asserted by John Wallace.
Aug. 3, PETER MALONE (his mark), formerly of Philada.,

1780.

breeches-maker, who hath lived in New York near five years & lately escaped to this City.

Aug. 4, NICHOLAS EGGERS, a Brittish Soldier, pressed in England, & deserted from Charlestown.

16, ABRAHAM FORST, Mercht., lately arrived in this City from Eustatia.

17, JOHN PATRICK LYNCH, Mercht., lately from the Kingdom of Ireland.

Sept. 22, WILLIAM DEWEES proves that he took the Oath of Allegiance in the year 1777 before me.

Oct. 4, MARCUS IOANE (his mark), Seaman, a Venitian by birth, arrived lately from Guadelope & has been some time in the Marine Service of this State.

10, JAMES SMITH, of the Forage Department, affirms that he took the test as by law directed in the year 1777, & had a certificate from me, which is lost.

JOSEPH NOURSE, of Philada., proved that he took & subscribed the Oath as by law directed in the year 1777.

Nov. 13, ALEXANDER BRODIE (his mark), Seaman, a native of Scotland lately arrived in this State from the Island Eustatia.

Dec. 13, HUMPHREY WILLIAMS, of Northern Liberties, Philada. Co., proves by Original Certificate, that he took & subscribed the Affirmation of Allegiance, the 1st of July 1777.

1781.

Jan. 11, GEORGE HOOK (his mark), born in Philada., a seaman having been some time a prisoner in New York, from whence he is lately discharged.

1781.
Jan. 27, MICHAEL CAIN (his mark), deserted from the Brittish Service in the year 1779. Labourer.
Feb. 3, THOMAS BECK (his mark), of Philada., shoemaker, proves that in the year 1777 before me he took and subscribed the Oath as by law directed.
March 1, CHRISTOPHER CLARK, Carpenter, lately arrived from a three years captivity in England, being a native of Boston.
    3, CONRAD KELLER, a Switzer, enlisted with the Brittish, deserted in Philada., & now following the trade of tinker.
   12, HEINRICH SCHMITT, a Hessian formerly in the Brittish Service, since in the American Artificers & discharged; by trade a Joyner.
   13, DANIEL BECKLEY, Carpenter, by Original Certificate No. 274, proves that he took the test to this State, according to the Act of 13th June 1777, the 30th day of the same month.
      JAMES BELL, of Philada., Carpenter, by Daniel Beckley proves that he took the test of the 13th of June 1777 before me, in July of the same year.
   31, ALEXANDER LOUIS O'NEILL, a native of France, late Captain in Genl. Count Pulaski's Legion.
April 19, ISAAC DAVIS, late of Harford Township, Chester County.
May 1, CHRISTOPHER FREDERICK DIEFFENBACH, by birth a German, arrived in this City about 18 months since; by trade a butcher.
   15, POWEL ADAM GARDENOK, a German Anspacher,

1781.

tinman & brazier, deserted from the Brittish near New York, about a year past.

May 28, JOHN MOYLAN, a native of Ireland, lately arrived in this City from the Camp of General Washington.

June 23, JOHN DAVID CRIMSHEW, Attorney at Law, late of New York.

25, JOHN PLEINY, a German by birth, lately arrived in this State and was a prisoner in England; taken on his way, being bound to Boston.

26, JOHANNES MARCUS (his mark), a native of Denmark, by trade an Instrument maker & turner; lately arrived in this state.

July 7, JAMES DAVIDSON, proves that about the month of June 1777, then being a professor in the College of Philada., he took the Oath of Allegiance & Fidelity as directed by law.

20, CHARLES ISAAC, arrived in the Brig Burton, from Charlestown. Mariner.

21, FREDERICK CHRISTIAN, of Philadelphia, Baker, by Bethenah Hodgkinson, proves that he in the year 1777, before me took & subscribed the Oath of Allegiance.

30, JOSEPH DOLBY, of Philada., Shoemaker, proves by Isabella Rogers that he in the year 1777 before me took & subscribed the Oath of Allegiance.

Aug. 28, HENRY HUDSON, late of Virginia. Wheelwright.

Oct. 1, JASPER ALEXANDER MOYLAN, late from the Kingdom of Spain. Student in Law.

9, JOSEPH GRAY, proves by William Gray that he took

1781.

(71)

& subscribed the Oath as directed by the Act of 1777 & had a Certificate, which is lost.

Nov. 5, WILLIAM AUSTIN SMITH.
ROBERT DOWNS, born in Philada.
BENJAMIN CARR.
CHARLES DECOSTER (his mark).
LEWIS DESANTEE (his mark).
BRYAN HYNES.
THOMAS MURPHY.
WILLIAM CODD (his mark).
} These 8 except Robert Downs are foreigners, Seamen, & now residenters in this State.

(JOHN GILCHRIST), a blackman. Deferred.

20, HENRY MEVINS, a soldier in the Brittish service, deserted about two years ago.

Dec. 26, JOHN GRIMES, formerly in the American Marines, taken prisoner by the Brittish & entered into that service; since taken by the Americans.

27, NICHOLAS ESLING, lately deserted from within the lines of the Brittish at New York.

1782.
Jan. 3, ANTONY MARSHAL, late a prisoner with the Brittish, a Seaman, native of Sicily, taken at Sea in an American Privateer.

16, SAMUEL MONTGOMERY BROWN, of the Kingdom of Ireland, lately arrived in this City from the Island of St. Thomas.

22, MARCUS MCCAUSLAND, of the Kingdom of Ireland, Mercht., lately arrived in this City from the Island of St. Thomas.

23, DANIEL ACKLEY, by trade a Carpenter, a native & inhabitant of N. York, deserted from thence and lately come to this City.

1782.
Jan. 23, THOMAS PETTIT, a native of New York & an inhabitant, deserted from thence & lately arrived in this City; by trade a Silver Smith.

30, GEORG HUBER, an Anspacher, in the Brittish Service, deserted in the year 1778, when in this City & hath continued in this state ever since; by trade a taylor.

Feb. 12, WILLIAM WILSON, formerly in the American Army in Canada, taken by the enemy, escaped from them and brought prisoner to this City & discharged by the Board of War; by trade a hatter.

JACOB CALB (his mark).
JOHANNES MAYER (his mark).
} Deserters from the Anspach troops, before the surrender of the Brittish Army in Virginia.

21, BENJAMIN JAMES MARCER, formerly a resident of this State, lately from New York; by trade a Shoemaker.

22, GEORGE LARRISON of Cohansey in the State of New Jersey; turner.

JAMES COLLINS, Mercht., late of the Kingdom of Ireland, & lately come to this City from New York.

ALEXANDER SEMPLE, lately arrived in this City from Jamaica by way of New York. Mercht.

March 13, WILLIAM ATCHISON, Mariner, a native of Scotland, from the Island of St. Thomas.

April 2, CHARLES STILWIL, a native of New York, lately from Bermuda.

1782.

April 2, JOHN HAMILTON, a sea-faring man, born in Ireland; last from Bermuda.

4, JAMES GENTLE, now of Philada., Bookbinder, was a prisoner in England & beyond the sea until within about a year last past.

THOMAS NEWARK, late an Inhabitant of Salem Co., now of the City of Philada. Taverner.

HENRY SPARKS, late of Salem County, now an Inhabitant in Philada. City Corder.

5, NICHOLAS KIRWAN, formerly an inhabitant of Antigua, lately of the City of Philada.

NICHOLAS DEERING, formerly an inhabitant of Antigua, lately of Philada. Mercht.

10, CORNELIUS BARNS (his mark).
RICHARD PERRY (his mark). alias Tempest.
JAMES HURST (his mark).
} Three soldiers deserted the British Army, now on the Staten Island, examined by Council and admitted.

15, GEORGE OLIVER, a Seaman taken prisoner into New York, late a pilot of the river Delaware, deserted the Brittish Service at Charlestown and arrived in Philada. in September last.

17, JOHN HERBERT GRUBB.
ISAAC KING (his mark).
JOSEPH MAYNARD.
} Deserters from the Brittish Army at N. York; recommended by Secty. Matlack.

May 4, JOHN HENRY, formerly of Philada., taken prisoner in the Brittish Service in South Carolina.

1782.
May 8, LUKE THOMAS, formerly of Philada., latterly of New York; returned by permission from the Council of this State.
    9, DANIEL MONTGOMERY, Taylor, deserted from the Brittish Army in Philada. in 1777.
       GEORGE HINTON, born in Philada., apprentice to John Fox, taken away with the Brittish, taken prisoner and now discharged.
    13, GEORGE INGLIS, lately from Jamaica by way of New York.
    15, PATRICK LANDERKEN (his mark), formerly in the Brittish Mercht. Service; by trade a Cooper.
June 7, CORNELIUS DEY, a seaman deserted from the Brittish Service.
       JEREMIAH MURRY (his mark), a seaman deserted from the Brittish Service.
    11, JOHANN ROTHMANN, deserted from the Brittish Infantry in the year 1778.
    12, ROBERT MCCAUSLAND, lately from Antigua, by way of New York. Mercht.
    29, WILLIAM MONTGOMERY BROWN, Mercht. from Ireland to New York, and to Philada. with a flag.
July 2, WILLIAM PETERS JUNR., of this City, taken prisoner by the Brittish in the year 1777; taken at sea.
       (CAPT. JOHN MCNACHTANE) took and subscribed the Oath of Allegiance the 30th day of June 1777, as appears by Original Certificate. No. 330.
    10, JAMES STEEL, formerly in the Brittish Service taken at Yorktown & discharged; by trade a Sadler.

1782.

July 10, John Kenedy. ⎫ Deserters from the Brittish,
John Fitzpatrick   ⎬ permitted by Council to con-
(his mark).   ⎭ tinue in this State. La-
                        bourers.

    Patrick O'Donnell, lately from New York & permitted by the president.

16, Silvester White (his mark), lately deserted from the Brittish on York Island; permitted by the Presdt.

29, John Keyser, deserted from the Brittish Army & Hessian line 4 years past.

Aug. 3, William Blake, an inhabitant of Boston, on his way to Newburyport, express for Donaldson & Co.

    Timothy Hickey, says he deserted the Brittish Service about four years ago.

5, John Wright, deserted from the enemy about three years ago; by trade a Hoosier.

    James Stokes, deserted from the enemy, hath resided in this City above two years; a dealer in goods.

    Samuel Read (his mark), deserted from the Brittish about eighteen months since; a wool card maker.

    Abraham King (his mark), deserted from the enemy & hath resided in Philada. four years; wool comber.

    John Moore, deserted from the enemy about a year & followed his trade of Taylor in Philada.

    Christian Bush (his mark), deserted from the enemy about 4 years. Cheap fitter in Philada.

1782.
Aug. 5, CHARLES DANIEL BOOS, deserted from the enemy about 4 years and kept store in Philada. the last year.
    GEORGE HERFFORD, deserted about nine months from the Brittish Service; by trade a Silversmith.
    JOHANNES LOOMSBACH, deserted above two years from the Brittish Service and hath resided that time in Philada. Hostler.
    MARTIN CHRIST (his mark), deserted the Brittish Service above four years; by trade a Hozier.
6, JOHN BROWN, deserted the Brittish Service about 4 years ago from the Hessian line.
    CHARLEAS HEATLY, lately from St. Christophers; Barrister at Law.
    PETER KEMBLE, from St. Christophers, Mercht.
    HUGH MOORE, from St. Christophers, Mercht.
    JACOB JARVIS, from Antigua, Mercht.
    THOMAS MCCLENNEY, from Antigua, Mariner.
    GEORGE READ, from Antigua, Clark.
    CONRAD HANKEL, late in the Brittish Service, a waggoner & came to this City, about 4 years ago.
    FRANCIS KREANING, deserted the Brittish Service & Hessian Line at the Battle of Monmouth; Shoemaker.
    JOHN SHEE, deserted above three years from the Brittish Service; hair dresser.
    HENRY DEWERS, deserted the Brittish Service above three years; shoemaker.
    VALENTIN SCHMITT, deserted the British Service about four years; a barber.

1782.

Aug. 6, FRANCIS OTTO, deserted the Brittish Service about 4 years, a Hessian; by trade a book-binder.

JOHANNES PARKMANN, deserted the Brittish Service & Hessian Line about one year; by trade a tanner & currier.

JOHANN BISHOP, deserted the Brittish Service & Hessian Line about one year; by trade a Shoemaker.

GEORGE TODD, deserted the Brittish Service in 1777, by trade a Barber.

FERGUS McCREA (his mark), deserted the Brittish Service about two years. Labourer.

JAMES McMILLEN (his mark), deserted the Brittish Service near 4 years; by trade a Mason.

PETER BRUCE (his mark), deserted the Brittish Sea Service about six weeks; seaman.

ADAM OPPERMAN, deserted the enemy & Hessian line about 4 years; by trade a Weaver.

JAMES RONALS, deserted the enemy about 2 years past; labourer.

FRANCIS REYNHART (his mark), a Hessian deserter from Virginia; labourer.

WILLIAM GARMAN (his mark), a Hessian deserter from New York; Labourer.

7, CASPAR GOLDSCHMITT, a Hessian deserter from New York about 4 years past; schoolmaster.

ADAM CULLMAN, a Hessian deserter from New York lately; Shoemaker.

JOHAN MICHAEL AIRHOTT, deserted the Brittish & line of Anspach 2 years past.

1782.

Aug. 7, FREDERICK GRUNWOLD, deserted the Brittish & Hessian Line from Virginia above one year; a Baker.

HENRY BLATTERMAN, deserted the Brittish and Hessian Line about 3 years from New York; a Baker.

PHILIP SMITH.

JOHN DURIE (his mark), deserted the Brittish & Hessian Line above 3 years; Labourer.

DANIEL BENDER (his mark), deserted the Brittish & Hessian Line above 4 years past; labourer.

KENETH MCLEAN, a Scotchman, deserted the Brittish at the Battle of Monmouth; labourer.

JOHN REYNARD (his mark), deserted the Brittish from Virginia about two years; Labourer.

RICHARD MCGREGOR (his mark), a Scotchman, deserted the Brittish at Stony Point in 1779.

ARTHUR BARNS (his mark), an Irishman, deserted the Brittish at Camden in Carolina in 1780.

JOHN MARTIN ZIPOLT, deserted the Brittish & Hessian Line at the Battle of Monmouth; Barber.

GEORGE KEIDEL (his mark), deserted the Brittish on Long Island in April last; Baker.

PETER DAVIS (his mark), deserted the Brittish Army and Hessian line at Kingsbridge last month.

WALDROP SIEMAN, deserted the Brittish Army & Hessian line at Kingsbridge, 4 years past. Wheelwright.

GODFRIED WASPHAL, deserted the Brittish at Gloster, a Hessian; Hozier.

1782.

Aug. 7, JACOB RANGANER (his mark), an Anspacher deserted the Brittish at Kingsbridge near 3 years; Taylor.

JOHN LEWIS (his mark), deserted the Brittish at Kingsbridge, February last, a Hessian; labourer.

BERNHARD KOEHLER, a Hessian, deserted the Infamous Arnold last year; loom weaver.

ANTHONY GEORGE, deserted the Brittish Army & Line of Waldeckers about 4 years past; a pedler.

WILLIAM KOY (his mark), deserted the Brittish Army in Virginia about one year past; labourer.

TIMOTHY RUSSEGUE, an American, deserted the Brittish at Gloster in Virginia in 1781; labourer.

JAMES JACKSON, deserted the Brittish Army at Gloster in Virginia in 1781; labourer.

8, JAMES BOYLE (his mark), deserted the Brittish Army in 1778, a Scotchman; by trade a Weaver.

JOHN MCGREGOR (his mark), an Irishman, deserted the Brittish Army at Kingsbridge in 1778; labourer.

MICHAEL GEHRING, deserted the Brittish Army last fall from Canada; labourer.

DANIEL VOGEL, deserted the Brittish Army at St. Johns in Canada about a year past; labourer.

GEORG BRUNER, deserted the Brittish Service & Line of Anspach last fall; taylor.

JOHAN HARTLAN, deserted the Brittish Army & Line of Anspach from Virginia last fall; brewer.

JOHAN KLEIN, deserted the Brittish Service & Line of Anspach from Virginia last fall; blacksmith.

1782.

Aug. 8, JOHN ROBERT (his mark), deserted the Brittish Service & Hessian Line; labourer.

JAMES MCMULLEN, deserted the Brittish Army from York near 3 years past; labourer.

LEWIS ILGEN, deserted the Brittish Service & Line of Anspach from Kingsbridge; labourer.

WILLIAM ESENBECK, lately deserted the Brittish Service and Line of Anspach; labourer.

GOTFRED SOYTDER, deserted the Brittish Service & Hessian Line three years past; wheelwright.

BALTUS SCHUNEL, deserted the Brittish Service & Line of Anspach in 1778 from Rodessland; House carpenter.

9, GODFREY ROSENBERGER (his mark), deserted the Brittish & Line of Hessians at Kingsbridge about a year past; butcher.

JOHANN SCHEILER, deserted the Brittish at Fort Ann & the Hessian Line at Fort Ann above five years past; labourer.

PETER LEECH (his mark), deserted the Brittish Army from Jersey in 1778; labourer.

AUGUSTUS KAJE, deserted the Brittish Service & Hessian Line above two years past; Shoemaker.

LUDWIG MEAYN, deserted the Brittish Service & Hessian Line from Jersey last year; wheelwright.

FRIEDERICH MIDDLEHAUSER, deserted the enemy & Hessian Line at Kingsbridge in Nov. 1779; Skindresser.

EDWARD RYAN, deserted the Brittish Army at Monmouth in 1778; hairdresser.

1782.

Aug. 9, CHRISTIAN MULLER, deserted the Brittish Service & Hessian Line in Virginia in 1781; Gardener.

GEORGE ESHRICK (his mark), deserted the Brittish Service and Line of Anspach in Virginia this year; gardener.

GEORGE STEAR, deserted the Brittish Service & Hessian Line at New York above two years past; a baker.

WILLIAM MCDONALD, deserted the Brittish Army at New York in Decr. 1781; Taylor.

10, CHRISTIAN KAUCH, deserted the Brittish Service, a Brunswicker, in the year 1781; labourer.

CHRISTOPHER ARMSTRONG, deserted the Brittish Army at Monmouth in the year 1778; labourer.

FRANCIS REED (his mark), deserted the Brittish Army at Virginia, May 17th 1782; labourer.

HEINRICH WIEST, deserted from the Brittish Service & Hessian Line at Germantown in 1777; Shoemaker.

CHRISTIAN FRIEDERICH REINBOTT, deserted the Brittish Service & Hessian Line at Kingsbridge in February 1782; Shoemaker.

GEORG ADAM ALBERT, deserted the Brittish Service & Hessian Line from Virginia last year; Locksmith.

ANTHONY POWELL, deserted the Brittish Service & Hessian Line at Kingsbridge in 1781; Sadler.

RICHARD MANDRY, deserted the Brittish Army in North Carolina in 1781; Shoemaker.

1782.
Aug. 10, WILLIAM HOOK (his mark), deserted the Brittish Army in the Jersey State 1778; Weaver.

CHARLES HAZLEY, deserted the Brittish Army in Virginia, August 1781; Labourer.

HEYNRICH HEYNEMAN, deserted the Brittish Service & Line of Anspach at York, Virginia in 1781; Potter.

BALTHAZER DILL, deserted the Brittish Service & Line of Hessians at Brandywine in 1777; Blacksmith.

JOHANN VALTIN EDELING, deserted the Brittish Service & Line of Hessians at Kings Bridge in the year 1781. Wheelmaker.

12, LEWIS PRICE (his mark), deserted the Brittish Service & Hessian Line in Jersey 1778. Labourer.

THOMAS WILLIAMS, deserted the Brittish Army in North Carolina in 1781. Shoemaker.

VALENTIN BUCHHOLTZ deserted the Brittish Service & Line of Hessians at New York about two months past. Miller.

JAMES DUNBAR (his mark), Deserted the Brittish Army in Jersey in 1778. Labourer.

LUDWIG DUDENGÖSS, deserted the Brittish Service & Hessian Line at Kingsbridge in 1781. Labourer.

HENRY HEIZER (his mark), deserted the Brittish Service & Hessian Line, at Charles Town in 1781. Labourer.

PHILIP KÖHR, deserted the Brittish Service & Hessian Line at Benington in 1778. Skindresser.

1782.
Aug. 12, LAWRENCE EDDLESTON, Deserted the Brittish Sea Service from the Renown in 1779. Cheesemaker.

GOTTLIEB ANTON, deserted the Brittish Service & Hessian Line at Stony Point in 1779. Labourer.

GEORG RUMEL deserted the Brittish Service & Line of Anspach at Rhode Island in 1778.

THOMAS HINES (his mark), deserted the Brittish Army in Connecticut about three years past. Labourer.

CASPAR MILLER, deserted the Brittish Service in Virginia about one year, a Hessian; by trade a Weaver.

JOHANNES GIESSLER, deserted the Brittish Service & Hessian Line at New York March last. Weaver.

JOHN KNOWLES (his mark), deserted the Brittish Army at Virginia in 1781. Labourer.

MICHAEL DALLER, deserted the Brittish Army & Hessian Line at Germantown in 1778. Taylor.

JOHANNES OTTO, deserted the Brittish Service & Hessian Line in South Carolina in 1781. Weaver.

JOHN MUSTER, deserted the Brittish Service & Hessian Line at Staten Island about 3 years past. Weaver.

JOHANN LUTZ, deserted the Brittish Service & Line of Anspach at Virginia in 1781. Baker.

ANDREAS KIPP, deserted the Brittish Service & Hessian Line at New York about 2 months past. Weaver.

JOHANN GLICK, deserted the Brittish Service & Hessian Line at New York last month. Labourer.

1782.
Aug. 12, JOHN RICHHOWSER (his mark), deserted the Brittish Army in Virginia Septr. last. Tanner.

ERNST ENDESRUGGERN, deserted the Brittish Service & Hessian Line at Long Island three months past. Shoemaker.

CHRISTOPHER TILMAN (his mark), deserted the Brittish Service & Hessian Line at N. York three years past. Cutler.

HANCE KILLAMER (his mark), deserted the Brittish Service & Hessian Line at Kingsbridge last fall. Labourer.

HENRY MYERS, late Surgeon's Mate, deserted in May last from Long Island.

13, VANDEL STOUP (his mark), deserted the Brittish Service & Hessian Line at Kingsbridge, January 1781. Labourer.

JACOB FRANCIS, deserted the Brittish Army at Monmouth in 1778. Mason.

ROBERT MELVIN (his mark), deserted the Brittish Army at Charlestown in 1781. Labourer.

GEORGE WALKER, deserted the Brittish Army at Kingsbridge in 1779. Labourer.

JOHANN HEINRICH WAHL, deserted the Brittish Service at Kingsbridge in 1781. Shoemaker.

14, CHRISTIAN KEAVORT (his mark), deserted the Brittish Service & Hessian Line at Carolina Febr. 1782. Weaver.

GEORGE ANDERSON (his mark), deserted the Brittish Army at Virginia in 1781. Labourer.

JOHN MILLER (his mark), deserted the Brittish & Hessian Line in Philada. 1778. Labourer.

1782.

Aug. 14, JOHN SEMPLE (his mark), deserted the Brittish Service in England, came to America & served one year in the American Army. Labourer.

PETER FRANSES, deserted the Brittish Service & Hessian Line at N. York in June last. Barber.

GEORGE BURNHOUSE (his mark), deserted the Brittish & Hessian Line in 1781. Carpenter.

JOHN SPALTER (his mark), deserted the Brittish Service & Hessian Line in Jersey 1778. Labourer.

WILLIAM BERRY, deserted the Brittish Army at Statten Island in 1778. Labourer.

JOHN ATKINSON, deserted the Brittish Sea Service & Ship Hussar at New York in 1779.

FELIX PLAIN, deserted the Brittish Service at Georgia in 1781. Baker.

HEINRICH ALBERT, deserted the Brittish & Line of Anspach in Virginia in 1781. Taylor.

HENRY DEMD (his mark), deserted the Brittish & Hessian Line in Jersey in 1778. Labourer.

ZACARIAS PITTMAN (his mark), deserted the Brittish & Hessian Line at Jersey in 1778. Taylor.

THOMAS JACKSON (his mark), deserted the Brittish Army at New York in 1778. Brass founder.

JOSEPH WHITE deserted the Brittish Army at N. York 1778. Labourer.

HENRY HARRIS (his mark), deserted the Brittish Army at New York in July last. Labourer.

PETER SHUCHARD, deserted the Brittish Army & Hessian Line at N. York in 1779. Schoolmaster.

1782.

Aug. 14, MARTIN CASPER, deserted the Brittish Army & Hessian Line in 1778. Baker.

 GUSTAV CLARCK, deserted the Brittish Service & Line of Anspach in Virga. in 1781. Labourer.

 JOHN RUNDLEMAN (his mark), deserted the Brittish Army & Hessian Line at New London in 1777. Rope Maker.

 JOHN HARPER (his mark), deserted the Brittish Army at New York in 1780. Labourer.

15, JOHN ALBERT SHOVE (his mark), deserted the Brittish Service & Hessian Line in Jersey 1778. Labourer.

 WILLIAM SHELVOUGH (his mark), deserted the Brittish Army at Virginia in 1781. Labourer.

 FRIEDERICH SHUMAN, deserted the Brittish Army in Philada. in 1778. Labourer.

 JOHANN HEINRICH FRICHMAN, deserted the Brittish Service & Hessian Line in Jersey in 1778. Labourer.

 WILLIAM CONNELL, deserted the Brittish Sea Service from the Hunter Sloop at Sandy Hook in 1779. Weaver.

 JAMES ROBINSON, deserted the Brittish Army in Jersey in 1778. Weaver.

 JOHN BLAIN (his mark), deserted the Brittish Army in Philada. 1778. Labourer.

16, JACOB SHREIBER, deserted the Brittish Service & Hessian Line in Jersey in 1778. Labourer.

 WILHELM CASSELLMAN, deserted the Brittish Service & Hessian Line in Jersey in 1780. Labourer.

1782.
Aug. 15, JOSEPH CROOK (his mark), deserted the Brittish Army at Kingsbridge in 1780. Weaver.

THOMAS HOOKER (his mark), who deserted the Brittish Army at Monmouth in 1778. Baker.

MATTHIAS EIKHART (his mark), deserted the Brittish Service & Hessian Line at White Plains in 1778. Taylor.

BERNHARD SHAGERT, deserted the Brittish Service & Hessian Line at Philada. in 1778. Taylor.

FRIEDERICH BLOSS, who deserted the Hessian Line in Virginia in 1781. Taylor.

17, CONRAD LEITSHOK, deserted the Brittish Service & Hessian Line in March last from N. York. Weaver.

JOHANNES SAUTTER, deserted the Brittish Service & Hessian Line at Kingsbridge in July last. Baker.

GEORGE VENSELL (his mark), deserted the Brittish Service & Hessian Line at Kingsbridge in 1779. Taylor.

GEORGE STEPHNON (his mark), deserted the Brittish Service & Hessian Line in Jersey in 1778. Labourer.

JONAS HAVESSTRICK (his mark), deserted the Brittish Service & Hessian Line at Philadelphia in 1778. Labourer.

CONRAD GOTLIB (his mark), deserted the Brittish Army at the head of the Elk in 1777. Labourer.

TICTUS HUNTHEIMER (his mark), deserted the Brittish Service & Line of Anspach in Virginia 1781. Rope Maker.

1782.
Aug. 19, FREDERICK DEIMLING, deserted the Brittish Service & Hessian Line at Charlestown S. C. in 1780. Organ Builder.

 THOMAS SAMPLE, a Lieut., formerly in the Brittish Service, from which he was discharged in Philadelphia in 1777. Mariner.

 JOHN DOUGLASS (his mark), deserted the Brittish Army in Philada. in 1777. Labourer.

 JOHN ASSMUS, deserted the Brittish Army in Jersey in 1778. Locksmith.

 MICHAEL MCMAHON, deserted the Brittish Horse at Kingsbridge in 1779. Hairdresser.

 MAURICE BARNS, deserted the Brittish Army in S. Carolina in 1780. Taylor.

 SAMUEL CASEY (his mark), deserted the Brittish Army in S. Car. in 1781. Labourer.

 ROBERT TIVIMAN, deserted the Brittish Army from Paulus Hook in 1780. Shoemaker.

 JAMES BOYL, who deserted the Brittish Army at Dobbs' Ferry last month. Seaman.

 FRIEDERICH KORLODER, who deserted the Brittish Service and Hessian Line last winter.

 JOHN HAMILTON, deserted the Brittish Army & train of Artillery at Monmouth in 1778. Minor.

 ABRAHAM JAGGER, deserted the Brittish Army in Jersey in 1778. Weaver.

 JOHN COVE, deserted the Brittish Army on the Sarey in 1778. Smith.

 HEINRICH PRESUHN, deserted the Brittish Service & Hessian Line at Monmouth in 1778. Shoemaker.

1782.
Aug. 21, JOSHUA KELSEY, deserted the Brittish Army at Stony Point in 1779. Shoemaker.
JOHANN NIEMOND, deserted the Brittish Service & Hessian Line in Virginia 1781. Baker.
MARKS MCCARTY, deserted the Brittish Army at Long Island in the year 1782. Carrier.
JONATHAN CARLIN, deserted the Brittish Army & train of Artilery at Kingsbridge in 1779. Hozier.
GEORGE DERRY (his mark), deserted the Brittish Service & Hessian Line at Paulus Hook the 30th of last month. Labourer.
22, MATTHEW BALAM, took the Oath Decemr. 1778.
JOHN MAY, deserted the Brittish Army at Long Island in May last. Turner.
GEORGE HUGGINS, deserted the Brittish Sea Service from New York in April last. House Carpenter.
23, JOHN RITGIE, deserted the Brittish Service & Hessian Line in Jersey 1778. Carpenter.
24, DANIEL SINKET, deserted the Brittish Army in Jersey in 1778. Labourer.
26, BENJAMIN DOW, deserted from New York 18th inst. Blacksmith.
DAVID HOWELL (his mark), deserted from New York 18th Inst. Blacksmith.
27, THOMAS COX, Escaped from N. York the 18th Inst. Blacksmith.
JOHN MIDWINTER, Escaped from New York the 18th Inst. Blacksmith.
28, JOHN SPOONER, who deserted the Brittish Army at N. York the 15th Inst. Labourer.

1782.
Aug. 28, JACOB ZIMMERMAN, deserted the Brittish Service and Hessian Line in Virginia 1781. Weaver.
29, ADAM FRITENHEILER, deserted the Brittish Service & Hessian line in Virginia in Septr. last. Baker.
30, HENRY QUEERFORT, deserted Burgoyne's Army & Hessian Line in 1778. Carpenter.
JAMES BRUNTON, taken prisoner in the Brittish Service in Jersey in 1781. Surgeon.
31, PETER BLEIJER, deserted the Brittish Service & Hessian Line in Virginia Octr. 1781. Butcher.
PETER KEMMEL (his mark), deserted the Brittish Service & Hessian Line at N. York July 1782. Labourer.
Sept. 3, VALENTINE BORNMAN, deserted the Enemy & Hessian Line at Monmouth in 1778. Labourer.
5, WILLIAM ROBERTS (his mark), deserted the Brittish Army in Philadelphia June 1778. Labourer.
JAMES WIEAR, says he was prisoner with the Enemy 3 years & escaped from N. York 2 Inst. Taylor.
7, GEORGE BUCH JONES (his mark), says he deserted the Enemy at Canada from Carlton's Army in 1777. Carpenter.
FERDINAND WAGNER, says he deserted the Enemy in S. Carolina in 1781. Schoolmaster.
GILBERT HUNT (his mark), says he deserted the Enemy in Virginia, Inlisted in Maryland & is discharged. Labourer.
CONROD DEAN (his mark), says he deserted the Hessian Line at Fort Washington in 1771. Labourer.

1782.

Sept. 11, MATTHIAS HOHNERSN, deserted the Enemy & Hessian Line in Georgia in March last. Comb Maker.

 WILLIAM THOMAS (his mark), deserted the Brittish Army at Staten Island 8th Inst. Nailer.

 12, HENRY OSMOS (his mark), says he deserted the Brittish Army at Billingsport in 1777, a Hannoverian.

 13, SAMUEL SUMMERS, deserted the Brittish Army in Connecticut in 1779.

 23, KENNETH CAMPBELL, THOMAS BATLEY (his mark), deserted from the Enemy at Staten Island & from the 22nd Regt. Labourers.

 24, WILLIAM SMITH, deserted the Brittish Line from Staten Island 17th Inst.

 25, MATTHEW COULTHURST, lately arrived in this City from Nantz. Attorney at Law.

 JAMES BOWEN, an Inhabitant of N. Y. lately made his escape from thence. Joyner.

 FREDERIC GRANER, deserted the Enemy & Line of Anspach at York Island 15th Inst.

 JOHANN FRIEDELBACH, deserted the Enemy & Line of Anspach at York Island 15th Inst.

Oct. 3, PHILIP LYON, Ship Captain belonging to Philadelphia.

 7, WILLIAM MACPHERSON, Major in the American Army since Sept. 1779.

 8, JOSEPH ALSTON, a Native of Philada. in Martina, on publick Service from 1776 to 1781.

 WILLIAM HUCKEL, deserted the Brittish Service in Philada. in the year 1778. Upholsterer.

1782.

Oct. 8, JOHN DUGUID JUNR., an Officer in the Pena. Line in 1776, taken prisoner at fort Washington.

KENNEDY MCFARLAND, deserted the Brittish Service in Novemr. last.

GEORGE EDDY, lately arrived to the age of eighteen. Affirmed.

10, DANIEL BOLAND (his mark), deserted the Brittish at the White Plains in 1776, served in the American Navy & lately discharged.

14, DAVID DENNY, Midshipman on board the Mede Frigate New York 1st Octor. Inst.

19, WILLIAM WILLSON, deserted the Brittish Service into which he was prest when prisoner at New-York as he says.

WILLIAM DOWNEY (his mark), a prisoner at New York, pressed from the prison ship & deserted.

Nov. 2, JOHAN SCHNEIDER deserted the Brittish & Hessian Line near Kingsbridge in 1777. Surgeon's Mate.

5, HENRY HAMMER, deserted the Brittish Service & Hessian Line at Paulus Hook 1st Inst. Weaver.

HENRY OILL, deserted the Enemy from York Island the 1st Inst. Taylor.

FRIEDERICH SHMID, a prisoner of War, discharged by the Council of State.

10, CONROD LUTHER (his mark), deserted the Enemy & Hessian Line in Jersey in 1778.

13, JOHN ANDREW LUZER (his mark), deserted the Enemy & Hessian Line at Paulus Hook 2d Inst. Labourer.

CARL BEYER, who deserted the Enemy. Surgeon's

1782.

Mate in the Hessian Line 3 years past, now married & settled in Northampton.

Nov. 21, NICHOLAS DOWNING, a seaman from Maryland on his way to Rhode Island to which he belongs.

DANIEL PLATT, lately from Maryland on his way to Connecticut to which he belongs.

22, JOSEPH BIDGOOD, lately arrived from Charlestown. Dealer.

23, JOHN MCGOUEN (his mark), who deserted the Enemy at Staten Island in Octr. last. Labourer.

25, ALEXANDER MURPHY (his mark), late Corporal in the 40 Brittish Regiment, deserted at Staten Island 20th Inst. Labourer.

JOHN BURRAGE (his mark), late Corpl. in above regt., deserted same time. Weaver.

27, JAMES DAVIS, who deserted the Brittish Service at the head of the Elk in 1777. Labourer.

HENRY GRANT (his mark), says he deserted the Enemy & Hessian Line at York Island 19th Inst. Dyer.

30, ROBERT STEWART, Mercht., lately from Ireland.

JOHN MILLER, who deserted the Brittish Service & Hessian Line in Jersey 1778. Weaver.

Dec. 2, ROBERT SIM, who deserted the Brittish Army at New York the 13th Inst.

3, JOHN CULNAN, from the Kingdom of Ireland, Resident in America about two years.

5, JOHN BLACK, formerly in the Waggon Department of this State.

1782.
Dec. 5, WILLIAM KELLY, well recommended from State of New Hampshire.
  7, ANDREW COWIE, a prisoner taken by the Brittish at Pensacola. Escaped from N. York.
  FRANCIS MOUSSU DELONGUAY, native of France lately arrived in this City. Mercht.
  JOHN COFFMAN, from Maryland with a pass, by trade a tanner & currier.
  11, CHARLES RINALDI, from Boston with a pass, on his way to Baltimore on Station.
  JOHN LAYCOCK, a Frenchman with a pass, from Boston on his way to Baltimore.
  14, HENRY HAMILTON, lately arrived in this City from St. Kitts Via Edentown, N. Carolina. Mercht.
  16, JOHN MEARS (his mark), deserted the Enemy in S. Carolina in 1780. Labourer.
  17, CASPAR SCHMIDT, appears to have deserted the Enemy & Hessian Line at York Island in 1779.
  18, WILHELM SITZDORFF, of the 60th Brittish Regt., deserted at Long Island in October last.
  JOMEL MENTZ (his mark), of the 60th Regt., deserted at Long Island in October last.
  23, WILLIAM SCOTT, taken prisoner by the Brittish at Pensacola, escaped from N. Y. 19th Novr. last.
  26, JOHN SHIELDS, deserted the Enemy from on board the Lion Man of War at N. York 29th Novr. last.

1783.
Jan. 30, PAUL WEAVER, who deserted the Enemy & Hessian Line at Charlestown in 1780.

1783.
Jan. 31, SAMUEL FRASER, deserted the Brittish Army at New York the 25th Inst. Labourer.

DANIEL McCARTER (his mark), deserted the Brittish Army at New York 25th Inst.

Feb. 6, JAMES ANDERSON, deserted the Brittish from the lines of New York in 1779. Labourer.

17, HENRY MILLER, a Hessian prisoner liberated.

20, SOLOMON PENDLETON, belonging to the State of New York with a pass from Justice Van Tassel of Winchester, York State.

March 3, MAGNUS MILLER, } just arrived in this City after
WILLIAM MILLER, } absence of near eight years.

8, MARTIN HENRY SHOLTZ, a Prussian, deserted the Brittish Army about 4 years. Breeches Maker.

14, ANDREW ALBERS (his mark), of the Regt. of Reidezel, a Prussian, late prisoner of war liberated.

15, JOHN PIGISSON, seaman, made his escape from the Midstone Frigate at N. York.

April 1, JONATHAN DAVIS, of the County Cumberland, State of N. Jersey. Turner.

DANIEL SMITH, of said County & State. Carpenter.

3, ALEXANDER SHLOTMAN, a Hessian deserted from the Enemy at Rhode Island in 1779.

May 12, MARTIN SHETLER } Germans born, deserted the
(his mark), } Brittish Army at Long Island
MARTIN HAGER, } the 25th of April last.

16, JOHN CLAUDE LAODIE, deserted the Hessian Army, served with the French General & discharged.

1783.

May 28, JOHANNES STAIN BAUGH, ⎫ lately deserted the ene-
JUSTICE FLOAK, ⎬ my & Hessian Line
WILHELM RUDOLPH, ⎭ from New York.

June 5, JOHN KEYS, being taken prisoner & forced into the Brittish Service in 1782, deserted the Man of War last week.

JAMES NEVIL (his mark), formerly of Maryland, taken prisoner by the Brittish at sea, was forced into the Brittish Service & deserted the man of war last week.

9, JOHANNES SHUGHART, ⎫ deserted the Brittish Army
JACOB BAUMGART, ⎬ & Hessian Line at New York.

12, JAMES DELANY, lately from Ireland.

17, A. J. DALLAS, from the Island of Jamaica.
JOHN BENTLEY, Idem.

19, JOHN NASSAU, a native of Philada., but pressed into the Brittish Sea Service.

(THOMAS BELL, late apprentice), see Oath of 1778.

20, PARRY HALL, Printer.

21, BOGEN, DOCTR. ⎫ Late of the Hessian Line & lately
GROSSE, DOCTR. ⎬ from New York, being discharged.

24, CHARLES CRAWFORD, Barrister at Law, lately arrived in this City, from Antigua via New York.

25, JOHAN MARTIN HENDERICH, of the Hessian Line, lately from New York. Joyner.

July 11, JAMES MACOMBE, Mercht., late of London last from New York.

Aug. 18, STEWART GEORGE DALLAS, lately arrived from Jamaica. Attorney at Law.

1783.
Aug. 19, JAMES CARROLL (his mark), Seaman for some years.
  21, JOHN QUINLEN, formerly in the Sea Service, late Captain of the Privateer Brigg Halker.
  MARTIN MAHER, lately arrived in this City from Martinique via Boston.
  27, JOHANN GROBEY, of Anspach, lately deserted the Brittish at New York.
Sept. 10, HENRY CARLISLE, lately from Ireland, a house Carpenter well recommended.
  11, JOHANNES EBERT, deserted from the Hessian Army & resident in this state three years.
  18, ALEXANDER STEWART, lately deserted the Brittish Army at New York.
  24, HENRY WEEKES, formerly in the Brittish Service.
Oct. 9, JOHN MARSAN, a native of France. Mercht.
  14, JAMES JOHNSTON, a soldier discharged, made proof that he took the Oath of Allegiance in 1777.
  GEORGE MEADE, took the Oath in 1777 as by testimony appears.
  ZACHARIAH LESH, proves that he took the test before me in 1777.
  ROBERT MORRELL, an artificer in the American Service, discharged.
  EDWARD WHELAN, a soldier in Pennsylvania Line, discharged.
  ROBERT TAYLOR, of Philada. made proof that he took the test in 1777 before me.
  ROBERT SMITH, of Philada. took the test June 27 1777 before me.

1783.
Oct. 14, JAMES AMES, of Philada. Blacksmith, proves that on the 31st July 1777 he took the Oath of Allegiance before me.
Nov. 3, CHARLES HUNTER, lately arrived in this City from Hampshire in Britain. Bricklayer.
    21, JOHN VEDER, lately arrived in this City, a Native of Rotterdam. Mariner.
    28, JOHANNES CRESS, lately arrived here from Amsterdam, a Baker by trade.
Dec. 1, JOHN ADAM SEITZ, lately from Germany, by trade a Miller.
    5, ALBERT WARNICK, deserted the Brittish Army at New York. Sadler.
    DAVID TURNER, late a prisoner of the Brittish Army in this City, discharged.
    8, ZEMAN THOMAS REDE, Barrister at Law, lately arrived in this City from London.
    JOHN DAVAN, Merchant, arrived in this City with his family about 4 weeks from Dublin.
    15, JACOB LAHN, lately at Baltimore from Amsterdam. Linguister.
    GEORGE BENDER, a Hessian lately deserted from New York. Taylor.
    FREDERICK MOLINEUX, of Philada. Mercht., took the Oath of Allegiance 31st Augt. 1777.

1784.
Jan. 23, LEWIS HALLAM, lately arrived from Jamaica.
    31, WILLIAM THOMPSON, lately from Ireland. Mercht.
Feb. 10, ISRAEL GOETTE, } Hessians lately
    LOEDWICK HUVORT (his mark), } from New York.

1784.
March 1, PETER BARRIERE, a native of France. Mercht.
  5, JOHN HAMILTON, of Pennsylva., lately from London. Attorney at Law.
  22, PETER MARKOE, Gentleman, lately arrived in this City from the Island Santa Cruz.
April 8, FELIX BRUNOT, native of France & a resident in this City three years. Hair Dresser.
  12, JOHANNES FISHER, a Hessian formerly in the Brittish Service.
  THOMAS WHITE, formerly of the Brittish Army, now resident in this City. Shoemaker.
  RICHARD HOWELL, Attorney at Law, a resident of the Jersey State.
  14, THOMAS CARSTAIRS, lately from London. House Carpenter.
  15, JOSEPH ALLENSPACHERN, lately from Germany. Clockmaker.
  21, JOHN MCINTOSH, lately arrived from Scotland.
  JAMES WILLIAMSON, same.
May 28, JOHN D. HAUSSMAN, a Dantzicker, lately from London. Mercht.
June 14, ARCHIBALD BLEAKLY, lately arrived from Ireland, says about 15 months. Mercht.
  17, JOHN ROOF, late of the County of Bucks. Blacksmith.
  ISAAC FRANK.
  HENRY GREER, late Lieut. of the 4th Pennsa. Regt.
  DAVID RITTENHOUSE, affirmed that in 1777, he took & subscribed as by law required.
  29, JOSEPH DE LA CROIX, a native of France, arrived here in January last.

1784.
June 30, CHARLES VAN ECKHENT, a Hollander by birth, bred in France & resident in America 4 years.

(REV.) JOHN CAMPBELL, of the Episcopal Church, lately arrived in this City from London.

July 5, STEPHEN SICARD, a native of France & a resident in this State 18 months.

JAN CHRISTIAN BRUYN, Cook, of Saxe Gothia resident here one year.

FREDERICK WILLIAM WINCKLER, Farmer, late of Germany & resident here six months.

8, GOTTLIEB KINDER, a German in the Brittish Service, deserted from Long Island.

14, JOSEPH HARRISON, formerly a subject of Britain lately from Charlestown. Mercht.

THOMAS VICKERS, formerly in the Brittish Service, lately arrived in Philada. Taylor.

19, JEAN KROP, a German discharged from the French Army, by trade a Joyner.

Aug. 6, CHRISTIAN GOTTLIEB BEMÉ, a Saxon, a resident 3 years in America.

18, MAXIMILIAN LOUIS ALEXANDER DE CRESSY, a native of France & resident in Philada. one year. Mercht.

24, JOSEPH HONAKER, of Moyamensing, & a Native of this State. Lately come to the age of 21 years.

Sept. 28, VINCENZO MARIA PELOSI, arrived in this City about a year past. Mercht.

Oct. 1, EDWARD ALLEN, Mercht., arrived about five months from Jamaica.

JOHN PHILLIPS, hairdresser, left Philada. in 1776 & returned in 1783.

1784.
Oct. 1, GUY BRYAN, arrived in this City from England in
Septr. 1783. Mercht.
WILLIAM FALKENER, Mercht., arrived in Philada.
in March last from England.
5, WILLIAM STILES, arrived in this City from London
above one year.
7, ROGER PRESCOTT, Mercht., arrived in this City from
London in Febry. 1784.
8, WILLIAM CAVENOUGH, Conveyancer, took the Oath
in Virginia in 1778.
9, JOHN LENTZ (his mark), son of Henry Lentz of
Moyamensing, lately arrived to age.
JONATHAN WORRELL, Cabinet Maker, took the Oath
in 1777 as appears by Certificate worn out.
CALEB EVANS, son of David Evans of this City,
lately arrived to Age.
JAMES HALL, a native of Moreland lately arrived
to full age.
DANIEL BOINOD, a foreigner resident of this City a
full year.
ALEXANDER GAILLARD, resident as above.
DAVID EVERHARD, Butcher, made Oath that he
took the Oath of Allegiance in 1777.
11, JOHN GUIER, son of Adam Guier of Kingsessing,
lately come of age.
ROBT. SMITH JUNR., son of Robt. Smith, lately come
to age.
BENJAMIN ROGERS, a Native lately arrived to the
age of 21 years. Shoemaker.
12, PETER REINHARD, Son of Martin Reinhard of

1784.

Passiunk, lately come to age of 21 years. Wheelwright.

Oct. 12, PETER STANLEY, son of the late Vale. Stanley of Philada., a freeholder.

BARTHOLOMEW SIMS, a native of Chester County, served Apprenticeship in this City, now 21 years of Age.

PETER FIELD, makes Oath that he took the Oath agreeable to Law in 1777.

JACOB GARAND, of Philada. Taylor.

JOHN SADLER, a native of Philada. lately come to age of twenty one years.

ANDREW SPENCE, Dentist, arrived in this City from London in July last.

JAMES HOGGEN, late of the State of New York, a resident in this City above three years.

ROBERT WATTS, of Philada. Cooper, made Oath that in 1777 in Bucks County he gave the test of Allegiance.

FREDERICK ESLING, son of Paul Esling of Philada., a native come to age of 21 years.

WILLIAM LEVERING, son of William of Roxbury, lately come to the age of 21.

JACOB MILLER, lately arrived to full age. A native of Germantown.

FREDERICK DOVER, a native of Philada. lately come to the age of 21.

JAMES TOD, arrived in this City from Edinburgh in Septr. 1783. Teacher of Languages.

THOMAS CRAIG, took the Oath in 1777 & had a Certificate which is lost.

1784.
Oct. 12, BENJAMIN ENGLE, a native of Germantown near 21 years of age.

PHILIP PELTZ, a native of Passiunk, now 21 years of age.

WILLIAM LOCKHART, arrived from Ireland, resident in this City above one year.

JACOB CUBLER (his mark), PHILIP YOUNG (his mark), natives of Passiunk & lately of the age of 21 years.

JOSHUA VANDEGRIFT, a native of Bucks County, lately come to the age of 21.

JOSEPH KEEN, a native of Philadelphia lately come to age.

CHARLES TODD, took the Oath in Maryland in 1777, resident 3 years in this City.

WILLIAM BROWN, arrived in this City from England near two years past.

NICHOLAUS DILL, formerly a Soldier in the Contl. Army & State of New York, a native of this City.

GEORGE DEAMAND, of Philada., Taylor, makes Oath that he took the Oath in 1777.

FRANCIS CUMFORT (his mark), a Seaman, has resided here two years.

THOMAS CLARK, resident in this city 4 years & lately come to full age.

WILLIAM MILLER, a native of Maryland & resident here above two years.

JAMES WILLIAMS, a native of Philada., took the Oath of Allegiance in Charlestown in 1778.

1784.
Oct. 12, FREDERICK JUDE, a residenter in Philada. from a Child, lately come to the age of 21 years.

ALEXANDER NIMMO, resident a full year. Shoemaker from Scotland.

THOMAS MCCULLEY, makes oath that he took the test of N. Jersey in 1778.

CORNELIUS BRADLEY (his mark), in servitude in 1778, lately arrived to the age of 25 years.

DONALD MCDONALD, a resident of Philada. who neglected to take the test in due time.

PETER VICTOR DOREY, a native of France, resident here above one year.

HENRY DETTERLINE, a native of Bucks County lately come to the age of 21 years.

ISAAC COATS, a native of the Northern Liberties, now 23 years of age.

JOHN LETCHWORTH, from England, resident here 15 years, lately come to full age.

WILLIAM YOUNG, son of a Freeholder of this City, late come to 21 years of age.

THOMAS A. MORRIS, from Ireland, resident above one year.

MATTHEW BROOKE, native of Philada. County, resident in this City lately. Affirmed.

JOSEPH MERCIER, a Foreigner, resident in this City three years. Mercht.

Nov. 22, JOHN CONRAD MITS, Wine Mercht. arrived in this City about 2 years past from Lubeck.

Dec. 9, JOHN CHILD, house Carpenter arrived in this City near two years past from England.

1784.
Dec. 13, JAMES BERWICK, late Lieut. in the Army of the United States, made Oath that in the year 1778 before Justice Hubley of Lancr., he did take & subscribe allegiance as by Law directed.

    17, (CAPT.) WILLIAM PINKERTON, of the Ship William & George.

    27, CHARLES PALESKE, lately arrived here from Dantzig. Mercht.

1785.
April 30, WILLIAM HEALY, Silver Plater, arrived from Dublin in November last.

May 9, WILLIAM NATHANIEL SWAIN, lately arrived in this City from Ireland.

    18, CARL DE DEKE, lately arrived from Germany, penmaker.

June 17, HENRY KESLER (his mark), a German, a resident of this state about six years.

    25, RICHARD LAKE, doctor of Law, lately arrived in this City from the kingdom of Scotland.

    JAMES STEVENS, arrived in this City about ten months from England. Mercht.

July 20, JAMES PRIDE, arrived here from Scotland in August last. Chandler.

    25, ZACHARIAH LOURIETTE, Mercht., from France, having resided here above eighteen months.

Aug. 9, JOSEPH ASHWORTH a native of Virginia. Farmer.

    17, CAPT. LEWIS GARANGER, a native of France, resident here & in the service of the States nine years.

    23, JOSHUA BYRON, from England, Mercht., says he has resided here above two years.

1785.

Aug. 23, THOMAS SEDDON, from England, Mercht., says he has resided here above two years.

25, HANDY PEMBERTON, (affirmed,) Barrister at Law, Lately arrived from Dublin.

Sept. WILLIAM JACKSON MCKENZIE, lately from Ireland. Mercht.

THOMAS O'NEILL, lately from Ireland. Mercht.

15, WILLIAM HUGH, Breeches maker, from Scotland, says above one year past.

26, JOHN DAVIS, Upholsterer.

JAMES KING, from Virginia, late of New York. Mercht.

29, LLOYD WHARTON, a native of this City lately come to the age of 21 years.

Oct. 8, PATRICK CONNELLY, says he was a Sergeant in the Maryland Line, was taken prisoner & inlisted in the Brittish Service & deserted from them in the year 1781.

WILLIAM YOUNG, Stationer, arrived in this City from Scotland in June 1784.

(ANNANIAS COOPER), swore allegiance 30th June 1777 as appears by a broken certificate.

GEORG KOOPER, proves that he took the test in 1777 & hath lost his certificate.

EDWARD MOYSTON, a foreigner, resident in this City above five years.

GEORGE MOORE, from Ireland, resident in this City near two years.

RICHARD PARKER, a native of this City lately come to full age.

1785.

Oct. 8, JOHN SELLERS JUNR., lately arrived to the age of 21 years.

THOMAS STEEL, son of David Steel, lately arrived to the age of 21 years.

THOMAS HOOD.

JAMES RONEY, from Ireland, arrived here about 18 months.

10, ABRAHAM KINTZING JUNR., a native of Philada. lately come to age.

EPHRAIM FERGUSON, from Ireland, resident in this City above one year.

ABSALOM THOMAS, a native of Bucks County, lately arrived in to full age.

JOHN CARRIN, maketh oath that he took the Oath in Cumberland Co. before Squire Loughlin in the year 1777.

JOSIAH W. GIBBS, came from Boston in the year 1779.

PETER BAYNTON, made Oath that he took Oath before me in 1777.

MATTHEW GRAHAM, made Oath that he took the Oath before me in 1777.

JOSEPH THOMAS, of Lower Dublin, lately come to full age. Affirmed.

WM. DONOVAN, from Ireland, resident of this City about two years.

PETER SCRAVENDYKE, Tallow Chandler, from Ireland, resident of this City two years.

WILLIAM COLLINS, Carpenter, from Ireland, resident here near two years.

1785.
Oct. 10, PETER WHITE, a native of this City, tinman, lately come to full age.

JOHN BRUNSTRONG from Sweden, resident here about 4 years.

11, JOSEPH MAFFETT (his mark), served apprentice in this City, lately of full age.

CHRISTOPHER SPITTER, a German, resident here near two years.

JOHN LACKRUM, makes Oath that he took the test in 1777.

JAMES RYAN, from Ireland, resident in this city above one year.

ALEXANDER MCDONALD, from Scotland, resident above one year.

SAMUEL SIMES, from London, resident above one year.

MARTIN KUBLER, lately come of age.

ECCLES BUCHANAN, from Ireland, resident here near two years.

SAMUEL LOWREY, of the Jersey State, lately arrived to full age.

JAMES WADE, native of Philada., lately come to full age.

THOMAS RANDALL, from London, resident here two years.

HENRY TOWN, a native of Philada., lately come to full age.

JOHN JOHNSON, from Ireland, resident here near two years.

GEORGE WHITE, from England, resident here near two years.

1785.
Oct. 11, JACOB ECKSTEIN, served apprenticeship here & lately come of full age.
 JOSEPH LAMBETH, from England, resident here near two years.
 ROBERT BREARLY, from England, resident here four years.
 WILLIAM MCDERMOTT, from the Jersey State, where he took the Oath of Allegiance in 1777.
 JOHN WILLSON (his mark), from Ireland, served apprentice in Chester Co. lately come to full age.
 FREDERICK BURKHARD (his mark), a native, served apprentice in Philada., of age near 4 years.
 JOHN WALRAVIN, a native of the Delaware State.
 JACOB TAYLOR (his mark), a native of Philada., lately come to full age.
 E. DOUGLASS, of Philada., Mercht., native of Penna., resident here 4 years & lately come to full age.
 JOHN GODSHALL, of Philada., now 25 years of age.
 SAMUEL HARKNESS, from Ireland, resident here above one year.
 ALEXANDER SYMINGTON, from Scotland, resident above two years.
 WILLIAM RICHARDSON, from Ireland, resident here above one year.
 RICHARD DENNY, a native of Philada., now 22 years of age.
 TIMOTHY RYAN, from Ireland, resident here near 27 years.
 CHURCH CLINTON, from Ireland, resident above one year.

1785.

Oct. 11, GILBERT GAA, a native, resident in Philada. where he served apprentice, lately of full age.

THOMAS MAYSEY, took the test in Jersey in 1777 & now before me.

BENJAMIN MCELROY, served apprentice in this City, late come to full age.

CHRISTIAN TULLON (his mark), from Germany when young, since resident of this State & lately come to age.

GODFREY TULLON (his mark), same.

CONRAD ROUN, took the test in New York in 1777 & now before me.

DANIEL PENINGTON, proves that he took the Oath before Justice Denci of Bucks Co. in the beginning of 1778.

EPHRAIM BROWN, makes Oath that he took the test in Rhode Island & now before me.

MAURICE DICKINSON.

DUNCAN MONTGOMERY, from Scotland, resident here above one year.

JOHN HUDSON, from the State of Virginia, resident in this City about 1 year.

WILLIAM SMITH, a native of Philada., lately come to full age.

JOHN GALVAN.

JAMES GARDETTE, from France, a resident in this City above one year.

ISRAEL ISRAEL, with Certificate from the Delaware State.

JAMES ROBERTS, took the test in Maryland in 1780 & now before me.

1785.

Oct. 11, THOMAS BREHNERT (his mark), from England near 2 years.

JOHN BAES, a foreigner, resident in this City near two years.

GEORGE HARMAN, a native of Phila la., lately come to full age.

CONRAD GARRETT (his mark), a soldier in the Penna. Line discharged on the peace.

GEORGE HARMAN, a native of this City, now of full age.

WILLIAM M. BIDDLE, a native of Philada., lately of full age.

JOHN LYNCH, a native of Virginia, resident in this City 2 years.

MARKS JOHN BIDDLE, a native of Philada., lately come to full age.

JOHN GOODMAN, a Native of Philada. Co., resident of Philada., lately come to full age. Affirmed.

JOHN McKINSEY, from Scotland, resident here one year.

JACOB LOWDEN, a native of this City, lately of full age.

PHILIP DEFRANCQUEN, from France, resident in this City above one year.

ABRAHAM BOYER, a native of Philada. County, resident of this City & lately of full age.

JOSEPH DAVIS, a native of Philada., son of a freeholder & of full age.

JAMES MACKAY (his mark), a native of Philada., lately come to full age.

1785.
Dec. 8, JOHN RICHARDS JUNR., Mercht., last from France, resident in this City above three years.

27, WILLIAM P. HARRISON, arrived in this City October 1784. Printer.

CARSTEN WINCKEL, lately arrived in this City from Amsterdam. Ship Carpenter.

1786.
Jan. 7, PETER LIGAUX, a native of France, lately from the West Indies.

Feb. 3, JOHN SAINTON, arrived in this City from Corsica about three years past.

FRANÇOIS SERRE, arrived in this City from France above two years.

VINCENT DUCOMB, arrived in this City from France above two years past.

HENRY STERNBAK, a German, arrived in this City near two years past.

March 17, ROBERT BUNTIN, a native of Ireland, resident in this City about 8 years.

April 3, JACQUE SALLIER, from France, resident here above two years. Taylor.

12, JOHN CRAWFORD, from Ireland, resident here above three years.

May 8, DAVID CLARK, from Scotland, resident near one year. Coachmaker.

ROBERT NICOL, from Scotland, Coach Maker, resident here near two years.

THOMAS LANG, from Scotland, resident here near two years.

JOHN FINETON, from Scotland, Carpenter, resident here above one year.

1786.
May 8, JOHN DUN, from Scotland, Carpenter, resident here near one year.
 JOHN ANDERSON, from Scotland, resident in this State one year.
 JOHN NICOLSON, from Scotland, storekeeper, resident in this City near two years.
 ROBERT JOHNSTON, from Scotland, Baker, resident of this State near two years.
 ROBERT OSWALD, from Scotland, House Carpenter, resident here above one year.
 JAMES COWAN, from Scotland, blacksmith, resident here above six months.
 ANDREW DUFFUS, from Scotland, Shoemaker, resident in this City Eighteen months.
 BENJAMIN JAMES, late of London, Mercht., resident in this City above two years.
June 6, ANDREW WERREBROUEK, late of Flanders, Mercht., resident here near one year.
 7, PETER L. CAILLEAU, late of Flanders, Mercht., lately arrived in this City.
July 11, ROBERT E. PINE, late of London, Painter, resident here about 2 years.
 12, JEAN BAPTISTE LEMAIRE, Mercht., from French Flanders, resident here above one year.
 ADRIEN JOSEPH LUBRER, from French Flanders, Mercht., lately arrived in this City.
Aug. 29, NICOLA MANSAI, hatmaker, arrived here from France one year past.
Sept. 2, THOMAS RYAN, breeches maker, from Ireland, arrived in this City about two years.

1786.
Sept. 23, JAMES REES, of Philada., lately arrived to full age.
  26, BENJAMIN H. SMITH, of the Township of Blockley, lately arrived to full age. Affirmed.
  30, THOMAS HURLEY, arrived in this City from Ireland above two years past.
Oct. 3, GEORGE RUDOLPH, of Philada., Rope Maker, lately arrived to full age.
  JOSEPH HODGSON, a native of the Delaware State, hatter, now near 20 years of age.
  JOSEPH KRESSON, of this City, Rope Maker, a freeholder, lately come to age.
  JAMES STEWART, arrived in this City from Ireland about two years, by trade a blacksmith.
  JOHN SNYDER, maketh Oath that in the year 1777 he took the Oath as by law directed before me.
  CHRISTOPHER FORD, Wheelwright, a Native of the City, lately come to Age.
  ROBERT PAISLEY, swears that at Bristol in Bucks County, he gave test of his allegiance in 1777.
  DAVID MCCALL (his mark), blacksmith, arrived in this City from Ireland about two years.
  9, LEONARD ALTEMUS, Taylor, a native of Philada., lately come to full age.
  JAMES ANDERSON, of Philada. Mariner, proves that he took the Oath in 1777 & had a certificate.
  JOSEPH MUSSI, from Italy, arrived in this City two years past.
  JOHN SUMMERS, Shoemaker, arrived in this City from Scotland two years past.

1786.
Oct. 10, BENJAMIN HARBESON JUNR., Mercht., lately come to age.

PETER THOMAS, Trader, arrived in this City from France above one year past.

FREDERICK HYNEMAN, by his Certificate shows that he took the test 30 June 1777.

ROBERT K. MOORE, of Philada., Mercht., lately arrived to full age.

WILLIAM FORGEY, Taylor, arrived in this City from Ireland three years past.

THOMAS ALBERTSON, of Philada., Skindresser, lately come to full age.

THOMAS SISSON, Conveyancer, arrived in this City from England above two years.

LEWIS EVANS of this City, silversmith, lately of full age.

CHRISTOPHER SMITH, proves he took the test in 1777.

JONATHAN SMITH JUNR., of Philada., Gent., lately arrived to full age.

GEORGE SMITH, Currier, arrived in America from Scotland above one year.

PHILIP DUNN, native of Philada., lately come to full age.

JACOB WONDERLY, of Philada., Butcher, lately come to full age.

WILLIAM OWENS, house carpenter, arrived in this City from Ireland above two years.

JABEZ EMORY, came to this City from Maryland when he took the test, resident here above 2 years.

1786.

Oct. 10, ALEXANDER GRANT, House Carpenter, arrived here from Scotland above two years.

ROBERT BLACKIE, blacksmith, come to this City above two years past.

WILLIAM SOTHERN, of this City, Mariner, resident here above one year.

ROBERT LUMSDEN, of Philada., Taverner, proves that he took the test in 1777.

ELIAS BOYS JUNR., of Southwark, a native lately of full age.

MANUEL ANTONY, native of Spain, Mariner, resident here five years.

THOMAS WYNN, of the Township of Blockley, lately come to Age.

JOHN CAROTHERS, taylor, arrived in this City about three years past.

CHAS. MCKIERNAN, Mercht., arrived in this City from Ireland full twelve months.

PATRICK GLYN, Taylor, arrived in this City above two years past.

OLIVER POLLOCK, of this City, Gent., arrived here from Havana near 2 years.

DAVID NEWEL (his mark), of Northern Liberties, lately come to full age.

JOSEPH JORDON, of the Northern Liberties, Plasterer, a Native lately come to full age.

JAMES HOOFMAN (his mark), of the Northern Liberties, Turner, lately come to full age.

MICHAEL HAINES, of the Northern Liberties, lately come to full age.

1786.
Oct. 10, JOHN MINGLE, of the Northern Liberties, Blacksmith, lately come to full age.
JOHN KINSEL, of the Northern Liberties, Blacksmith, native, lately of full age.
CADWALADER GRIFFITH, Shoemaker, lately come to full age.
LAURENCE LOTIE, barber, arrived in this City from France about 5 years past.
CHARLES DE GROFEY, Mercht., arrived here from France above three years past.
PETER ANDREWS, Cordwainer, a native of this City, lately come to full age.
WILLIAM BANDONINE, a native of New York, resident of this City two years, lately of full age.
JOHN FITZSIMONS, came to this City from Ireland about two years past.
WILLIAM FERGUSON, arrived here where he has resided near three years.
NICHOLAS HESS, Blacksmith, a Native of this State, lately of full age.
JOHN HESS, Blacksmith, a native of this State, lately of full age.
ELSHA HAGUE, a Native of Philada., lately come to full age.
12, JULIUS MANER, late a Hessian Soldier who hath served three years in the Army.

1787.
Jan. 31, JAMES YARD, a Native of this State, lately of full age.

1787.
March 3, THOMAS CRAIG, arrived in this City from Ireland in the year 1783, by trade a House Carpenter.
May 7, WILLIAM CUNNINGHAM, Stone Cutter, came to the City from London in the year 1783.
Sept. 6, ANGUS TAYLOR, Shoemaker, arrived in this City from Scotland above two years.

1788.
Sept. 19, GEORGE GREER, arrived in this City from Ireland in the year 1784.
    23, JOHN BRIGGS, Glover, lately from London.
    27, THOMAS COATS, Clock & Watch Maker, arrived in this City from Scotland in 1788.
Oct. 11, WILLIAM ANDERSON, of this City, hair dresser, who took the Oath of Allegiance in 1777.
    13, FREDERICK CONYNGHAM, arrived in this City in Septr. 1787. Mercht.
    14, JOHN SIMTER, formerly a Dragoon in the Service of the United States.
        JOHN EBALT, late a Soldier in the American Army.

INDEX TO HISTORY.

	PAGE
Adams, John, his resolution in favor of creating independent State Governments	xiii
Afflick, Thomas, arrested	xxi
Allegiance—Oaths and declarations of—For the support of British Government denounced by Congress—Grand Jurors' oath incompatible with opposition to the King	xiii
Religious test adopted	xiv
Justices of Peace oaths of renunciation and allegiance—Religious test for members of the State Assembly—Objections to it	xv
Testimony of Quakers against the test, December, 1776	xvi
State Navy Board refuses to take oath of allegiance to State—Offer to take oath in favor of United States	xvi
Test and oath of allegiance of 1777	xvii
Preamble to the act—Form of the oath	xviii
Penalties against persons who will not take the oath	xix
Whigs flock in to take the oath	xx
Time for taking oath extended	xxiii
Persons in certain professions prohibited from following them without taking the oath—Penalty for not taking the oath	xxiv
Protests of Quakers against the oath	xxv
Further extension of time to take the oath—Pardon of persons pertinaciously refusing to take the oath, 1778	xxvi
Opposition of Quakers to the test, 1779	xxvii
Proposition to abolish test laws, 1784, lost—Resolution to allow young men who arrived at 18 years since the passage of the law to take the oath—Referred to a committee	xxxiii
Non-jurors petition for rights of citizenship, referred—Proposition to exclude from citizenship all who aided the King of Great Britain in the late war, carried—Proposition to bring in a bill to entitle any one to take the oath of allegiance, carried—attempt to pass the bill—breaking up of the Assembly—nineteen members secede	xxxiv
Protest of the seceders—George Gray's (Speaker) address against seceders—reasons why test laws should be repealed	xxxv
Petitions by Non-jurors, 1785—General Anthony Wayne favors them,	xxxvi
Committee appointed—Bitter report against the Non-jurors	xxxvii
Arguments in favor of the oath—The report adopted—New petition of Non-jurors, 1785	xxxviii
Executive Council recommends abolition of the test laws—passage of Act of 1786 limited in terms	xxxix
Dissatisfaction of the Non-jurors—Remonstrances in 1787—Report of committee in favor of unconditional repeal—passage of an amended act—Quakers dissatisfied with it—Proceedings against two Grand Jurors	xl

	PAGE
Allegiance—Report in favor of repeal, 1788	xli
Final repeal of the test laws—Religious test in Constitution of 1776 repealed by Constitution of 1790	xlii
See also "Quakers," "Tories," "Associators."	
Allen, Andrew, attainted	xxiii
Allen, Jno., attainted	xxiii
Asheton, Thos., arrested	xxi
Ashmead, Samuel, candidate for Assembly, favorable to Non-jurors, 1784, defeated	xxxvi
Assembly of Pennsylvania under the crown—Distrusted at the commencement of the Revolution—Authorizes raising troops	vii
Measures taken to supersede it	xiii
Its dying protest	xiv, xv
Assembly of the State under the new Constitution	xv
Meets at Lancaster	xxii
Interrogatories to a committee of Quakers	xxiv
Queries to Quakers petitioning against test laws in 1779	xxvii
Unsatisfactory reply	xxviii
Broken up in 1784 upon attempt to pass laws for relief of Non-jurors	xxxiv
See "Allegiance," "Quakers."	
Associators—Volunteer militia	viii, ix
Dissatisfied with Assembly in 1776—Protest against allowing Assembly to choose their Generals—Circulars issued calling Convention at Lancaster	xii
Brigadier-Generals elected	xiii
In favor of suppressing old Provincial Assembly—Conference at Carpenter's Hall—Provincial Convention to form Constitution recommended—Religious test adopted	xiv
Not reliable troops—Desertions when at Amboy—City Troop at Princeton, N. J.—Superseded by militia under a general law	xvii
Attainder Act of 1778	xxii
Bergum, John, his recantation	viii
Biddle, John, attainted	xxiii
Bond, Phineas, arrested	xxi
Brown, Elijah, arrested	xxi
Byberry—Scarcity of persons who had taken the oath, 1785	xxxviii
Coats, William, elected to Assembly on anti-Non-juror ticket, 1784	xxxvi
College and Academy at Philadelphia—Charter taken away	xxii
Committees—City and County—Manage local affairs at beginning of Revolution	vii, viii
Committee of Inspection, Philadelphia, attack the authority of the King's Judges	xiii
Coombe, Rev. Thomas, arrested	xxi
Permitted to go to St. Eustatia	xxii
Confiscation of traitors' estates authorized	xxiii
Congress recommends formation of State Governments	xiii
Convention to frame Constitution—Proceedings of, 1776	xiv
Council of Safety appointed	xiv
Crathorne, Joseph, a Tory, ordered to leave Pennsylvania	xxxii
Drinker, Henry, arrested	xxi
Duché, Rev. Jacob Jr., attainted	xxiii

	PAGE
Eddy, Charles, arrested	xxi
Emlen, Caleb, arrested—Took the oath	xxi
Emlen, Samuel, Jr., arrested	xxi
Ewing, James, elected Brigadier General	xiii
Faro, Lancelot, a Tory, ordered to leave Pennsylvania	xxxii
Faro, Thomas, a Tory, ordered to leave Pennsylvania	xxxii
Fenner, Lawrence, a Tory, ordered to leave Pennsylvania	xxxii
Fisher, Jabez Maud, compelled to state who wrote a certain letter	viii
Fisher, Joshua, arrested	xxi
Fisher, Miers, arrested	xxi
Fisher, Thomas, arrested	xxi
Fitzsimons, Thomas, candidate for Assembly, favorable to Non-jurors 1784, defeated	xxxvi
Fouts, Christian, attainted	xxiii
Fox, Joseph, arrested	xxi
Francis, Tench, attorney for the Penn family, applies for restoration of their rights	xxxv
Franklin, Benjamin, President Convention to form State Constitution	xiv
President Supreme Executive Council—Recommended abolition of the test laws, 1785	xxxix
Fleeson, Plunket, Commissioner to receive oaths of allegiance	xxvi
Friends, see "Quakers."	
Galloway, Joseph, attainted	xxiii
Garrigues, Jacob, Assistant Secretary Convention to form State Constitution	xiv
Gibbons, Abraham, one of a Committee of Quakers	xxiv
Gilpin, Thomas, arrested	xxi
Dies in exile in Virginia	xxvi
Gratz, Bernard, of Jewish Congregation, protests against religious test	xxxii
Gray, George, Speaker of the Assembly, 1784—Censures the seceders	xxxv
Halliday, Robert, of Duck Creek, writes an obnoxious letter	viii
Hart, Joseph, Vice President State Conference	xiv
Hicks, Gilbert, attainted	xxiii
Howell, Isaac, Commissioner to receive oaths of allegiance	xxvi
Hunt, John, arrested	xxi
Dies in exile in Virginia	xxvi
Husband, Joseph, one of a Committee of Quakers	xxiv
Imlay, William, arrested	xxi
Released on parole	xxii
Jackson, James, one of a Committee of Quakers	xxiv
Jackson, Samuel, ordered to be arrested—Not found	xxi
Jackson, William Jr., one of a Committee of Quakers	xxiv
James, Abel, arrested	xxi
James, John, ordered to be arrested—Not found	xxi
Jervis, Charles, arrested	xxi
Jews—Protest against religious test in acknowledging the New Testament, 1783	xxxii
Jones, Norris, Quaker Grand Juryman, fined	xli
Jones, Owen, Jr., arrested	xxi

INDEX TO HISTORY.

	PAGE
Juncken. Herr, his recantation	ix
Justices of Peace appointed	xv
Keen, Reynold, attainted	xxiii
Knox, David, Commissioner to receive oaths of allegiance	xxvi
Kuhn, Dr. Adam, arrested—Produced proof that he had taken the oath—discharged	xxi
Lennot, William, arrested	xxi
Lennox, David, arrested	xxi
Levy, Mordecai, his recantation	viii
Lindley, Jacob, one of a Committee of Quakers	xxiv
Loosely, Thomas, is "exalted"	viii
McKean, Thomas, President State Conference	xiv
Chief Justice, fines two Quakers who had not taken the affirmation of allegiance	xl, xli
Marshall, Christopher, extract from his diary	viii
Matlack, Timothy, Secretary of Committee of Inspection	ix
Mifflin, Warner, one of a Committee of Quakers	xxiv
Miles, Col. Samuel, Chairman of a meeting against Tories, 1783	xxx
Militia law of 1777	xvii
Mitchell, James, a Tory, ordered to leave Pennsylvania	xxxii
Moderates agree with the views of the Tories	xiii
Moor, John, Commissioner to receive oaths of allegiance	xxvi
Morris, John, Secretary Convention to form State Constitution	xiv
Morris, Robert, his amendment to Act modifying test laws in 1786	xxxix
Morris, Samuel Cadwalader, Secretary State Conference	xiv
Murdock, Samuel, arrested	xxi
Myers, Asher, of Jewish Congregation, protests against religious test	xxxii
Nathan, Simon, President Jewish Synagogue, protests against religious test	xxxii
Oath—See "Allegiance."	
Ord, George, Commissioner to receive oaths of allegiance	xxvi
Ozeas, Peter, begs pardon for increasing price of coffee	ix
Pemberton, Israel, arrested	xxi
Pemberton, James, arrested	xxi
Pemberton, John, arrested	xxi
Penn, John, Senr., applies for restoration of his rights	xxxv
Penn, John, Jr., applies for restoration of his rights	xxxv
Penn, Richard, applies for restoration of his rights	xxxv
Pennington, Edward, arrested	xxi
Pettit, Charles, elected to Assembly on anti-Non juror ticket, 1784	xxxvi
Pike, Thomas, arrested	xxi
Pleasants, Samuel, arrested	xxi
Potter, John, attainted	xxiii
Putnam, Gen. Israel, his testimony as to inefficiency of Associators	xvii
Quakers, opposed to war and favor the Royal cause	v
Lose their power in Pennsylvania	vi

INDEX TO HISTORY. 125

	PAGE
Quakers—Testimony in favor of the King's Government, 1776—Satire upon American liberty in 1776	x
Testimony against tests and in favor of the King's Government, December, 1776	xvi
Complaints of seizures of their goods for military purposes—Their windows broken because they will not recognize public fast days—Abused because they would not illuminate their houses on the 4th of July—Quakers and Tories arrested by order of Congress	xx
Sent to Winchester, Va.	xxi
A committee ask leave to lay their sufferings before Assembly	xxiv
Queries as to their loyalty—Evasive reply—Protest by, against oath of allegiance	xxv
Petition for return of exiles in Virginia	xxv
Release and return of the persons who were banished	xxvi
Testimony of 1779 against the test laws—Memorial to the Assembly—Queries put by Assembly to the Quakers regarding their loyalty	xxvii
Evasive reply	xxviii
Dissatisfied with Act of 1786—Two Quaker Grand Jurymen fined	xl, xli
Quee, Seth, Commissioner to receive oaths of allegiance	xxvi
Rankin, James, attainted	xxiii
Rawlings, Captain Thomas, a Tory, ordered to leave Pennsylvania	xxxii
Richards, John, Commissioner to receive oaths of allegiance	xxvi
Roberdeau, Daniel, elected Brigadier-General	xiii
Roberts, George, arrested	xxi
Roberts, Hugh, arrested	xxi
Ross, George, Vice President Convention to form State Constitution	xiv
Salomon, Haym, of Jewish Congregation, protests against religious test	xxxii
Seixas, Ger, Rabbi of Jewish Synagogue, protests against religious test	xxxii
Shee, Lieut. Col. John, Chairman of a Meeting against Tories, 1783	xxx
Secretary of another meeting	xxxi
Shoemaker, Samuel, arrested	xxi
Attainted	xxiii
Sitgreaves, William, begs pardon for exceeding regulation price of coffee	ix
Smith, Jonathan B., Secretary State Conference	xix
Commissioner to receive oaths of allegiance	xxvi
Smith, Rev. William, arrested	xxi
Smith, William, (broker,) arrested	xxi
Smith, William Drewett, arrested	xxi
Stedman, Alexander, arrested	xxi
Stedman, Charles, Jr., arrested	xxi
Test, Religious, adopted by Conference of Associators	xiv
Tories—A powerful minority in Pennsylvania	vi
Kept down by committees	vii
Recantations by	vii, viii, ix, x
Favor the continuance of the Assembly of 1775-6, as State Government	xiii
Insolence of—Test and oath of allegiance demanded in consequence	xvii
Several Tories arrested by order of Congress—Sent to Winchester, Virginia	xx, xxi
Certain privileges guaranteed by Provisional Treaty with Great Britain—Resolves of the Philadelphia militia against them—Meetings concerning the same	xxx

	PAGE
Tories—Resolution that certain Tories shall withdraw from Philadelphia in ten days	xxxi
Tories—See "Quakers," "Allegiance," "Associators," "Assembly."	
Vernon, Nathaniel, attainted	xxiii
Warder, Jeremiah, arrested	xxi
Wayne, Gen. Anthony, favors the petitions of Non-jurors for repeal of test laws, 1785	xxxvi
The result	xxxvii
Wickersham, Amos, his recantation	vii
Wharton, Thomas, Senr., arrested	xxi
Young, James, Commissioner to take oaths of allegiance	xxvi
Young, Thomas, a Tory, ordered to leave Pennsylvania	xxxii

INDEX OF NAMES.

NOTE —*The names in italics are those who did not subscribe to the Oath, but who are mentioned incidentally.*

Name	PAGE	Name	PAGE
Ackley, Daniel	71	Armet, John	48
Adams, Christopher	59	Armitage, John	12
Adams, John	28	Armitage, Shewbart	53
Adams, Jonathan	24	Armstrong, Christopher	81
Adams, Thomas	28	Armstrong, James	16
Adcock, (Justice)	30	Armstrong, John	13
Ahl, Johan Peter	64	Armstrong, William	52
Airhott, Johan Michael	77	Arndt, Jacob	2
Aitken, Andrew	26	*Arnold, (Gen.)*	79
Akely, Abraham	12	Ash, Caleb	36
Albers, Andrew	95	Ash, Jacob	38
Albert, George Adam	81	Ashton, William	51
Albert, Heinrich	85	Ashworth, Joseph	105
Albertson, Thomas	115	Assmus, John	88
Alborn, Imanuel Jacob	48	Atchison, William	72
Albrecht, William	4	Atkinson, John	85
Albright, Jacob	6	Attkinson, George	3
Alenby, James	67	Avered, Seth	26
Alexander, Alexander	58		
Alexander, William	58	Backins, Godfrey	12
Allen, Edward	100	Baes, John	111
Allen, John	22	Baker, Christopher	4, 36
Allen, John	40	Baker, Jacob	19, 41
Allenspacher, Joseph	99	Baker, Johannes Hilarius	42
Alston, Joseph	91	Baker, John	26
Altemus, Leonard	111	Baker, Samuel	5
Ames, James	98	Baker, Samuel	20
Amos, Jacob	4	Baker, William	14
Amos, Jacob	5	Ballam, Matthew	24, 89
Amos, John	4	Bandomino, William	117
Anderson, George	81	Bankson, Jacob	14
Anderson, James	95	Bankson, William	30
Anderson, James	114	Barber, William	67
Anderson, John	11	Barclay, Alexander	11
Anderson, John	113	Barclay, John	11
Anderson, Joseph	31	Bardeck, Georg	59
Anderson, William	118	Bare, Jacob,	18
Andrews, John	4	Bare, John,	16
Andrews, Peter	117	Bare, John,	18
Anton, Gottlieb	83	Barge, Jacob	58
Antony, Manuel	116	Barnes, Cornelius	41
Appel, Daniel	21	Barnhill, Daniel	63
Apt, George	12	Barnhill, John Junr	56

INDEX OF NAMES.

Name	Page	Name	Page
Barns, Arthur	78	Bishop, Johann	77
Barns, Cornelius	73	Bitters, Charles	57
Barns, Daniel	66	Black, John	93
Barns, Maurice	88	Blackie, Robt.	116
Barns, William	37	Blain, John	86
Barr, Jacob	42	Blaine, Ephraim	28
Barriere, Peter	99	Blake, William	75
Bass, Robert	17, 36	Blatterman, Henry	78
Bastian, Wilhelm	43	Blatzer, Charles	61
Bates, George	36	Bleakly, Archibald	99
Batley, Thomas	91	Bleijer, Peter	90
Baumgart, Jacob	96	Bloss, Friederich	87
Baynton, Peter	58, 107	Blunt, Stephen	20
Beackley, Christian	8	Blutzer, Carl	14
Beaks, John	12	*Boatman, Philip*	66
Beale, William	43	Bogen, (Doctr.)	96
Bealer, David	56	Boinod, Daniel	101
Bealert, Jacob	37	Boland, Daniel	92
Becher, Jacob	4	Bolter, Joseph	48
Bechtel, Georg	10	Bond, George	23
Beck, John	17	Booker, Thomas	51, 66
Beck, Thomas	12, 69	Boos, Charles Daniel	76
Beck, Thomas	36	Bornman, Valentine	90
Beckley, Daniel	69	Bost, Jacob	14
Beckman, Johan Conrad	64	Boulter, Benjamin	13
Bedford, Gunning	8, 38	Boulter, Joseph	59
Bedford, Joseph	19	Bourne, Thomas	6
Bedford, Peter	19	Boutman, Philip	66
Beech, Edmond, Junr.	46	Bowen, James	91
Beekman, Gerard William	42	Bower, Charles	2
Bell, George	8	Bower, Francis	47
Bell, James	69	Bower, Jacob	64
Bell, John	5	Boyer, Abraham	111
Bell, Robert	20, 42	Boyl, James	88
Bell, Thomas	27, 96	Boyle, James	79
Bell, William	23	Boyle, Peter	13
Bemé, Christian Gottlieb	100	Boys, Elias, Junr.	116
Bender, Daniel	78	Bradford, William	24
Bender, George	98	Bradley, Cornelius	104
Benezet, Daniel	16	Brady, Samuel	27
Benner, Martin	3	Brand, Andrew	2, 36
Bensted, Alexander	28	Brearly, Robert	109
Bentley, Felix	46	Brehnert, Thomas	111
Bentley, John	96	Brethower, Cooper	47
Berry, William	85	*Brian, George*	40
Berwick, James	105	Brice, John	27
Beyer, Carl	92	Briggs, John	118
Biddle, Marks John	111	Brittin, John	10
Biddle, William M.	111	Brodie, Alexander	68
Bidgood, Joseph	93	Brooke, Matthew	104
Bigony, John	6	Brookes, John	15
Bigony, Joseph	6	Brown, Ephraim	110
Baron v Bilow, Carl Ludewig	66	Brown, Johann Conrad	5

INDEX OF NAMES. 129

Name	PAGE	Name	PAGE
Brown, John	37	Carrin, John	107
Brown, John	76	Carroll, James	97
Brown, Samuel Montgomery	71	Carstairs, Thomas	99
Brown, William	57	Carter, Thomas	9
Brown, William	103	Cartwright, Edward	14
Brown, William Montgomery	74	Caruthers, James	12
Bruce, Peter	77	Casey, Samuel	88
Bruner, Georg	79	Casper, Martin	86
Brunot, Felix	99	Cassellman, Wilhelm	86
Brunstrong, John	108	Caster, Jacob,	7
Brunton, James	90	Causten, Isaac	13
Bruyn, Jan Christian	100	Cavanaugh, Edward	41
Bryan, George	2	Cavenough, William	101
Bryan, Guy	101	Cecil, Charles	38
Bryan, John	19	Chain, William	7
Bryarly, John	26	Chandler, George	3, 37
Bryce, John	27	Channell, Samuel	56
Buchanan, Eccles	108	Channell, Thomas	63
Buchholtz, Valentin	82	Chapman, Benjamin, Junr.	53
Budden, William	13	Chevilier, Christian	11
Bulkely, Joseph	64	Child, John	101
Buntin, Robert	112	Christ, Martin	65, 76
Burgoyne, Gen.	90	Christian, Frederick	70
Burkhard, Frederick	109	Christy, James	5
Burklae, Jacob	11	Chrystie, James	27
Burly, Christopher	63	Chrystler, Jacob	10
Burn, Joshua	62	Clackner, George	20
Burnes, John	36	Clampffer, Adam	36
Burnhouse, George	85	Clarck, Gustav	86
Burrage, John	93	Clark, Christopher	69
Bush, Christian	75	Clark, David	112
Byron, Joshua	105	Clark, Michael	47
		Clark, Thomas	103
Cailleau, Peter L	113	Clark, William	42
Cain, Michael	69	Clark, William	55
Calb, Jacob	72	Clauzer, Philip	9
Calbanan, John	51	Clay, Jonathan	11
Caldwell, James	16	Claypoole, George	18, 27, 33
Campbell, John	52	Claypoole, James	4, 22
Campbell, John	100	Clazer, John	51
Campbell, Kenneth	91	Cleigner, Casper	51
Caner, Michael	51	Clinton, Church	109
Cannan, Thomas	5	Coates, John	43
CAREY, MATTHEW	30	Coats, Isaac	101
Carlin, Jonathan	89	Coats, Thomas	118
Carlisle, Henry	97	Cochran, William	4
Carlton, ――	90	Codd, William	71
Carns, John, Junr.	18	Coffin, Elijah	33
Carothers, John	116	Coffman, John	37
Carr, Benjamin	71	Coffman, John	94
Carr, James	18	Colewater, Philip	39
Carradine, Thomas	20	Coldlesh, Heinrich	17
Carrick, Jacob	36	Coldlesh, Mathias	17

R

INDEX OF NAMES.

Name	Page	Name	Page
Collins, James	72	Croghan, George	36
Collins, John	11	Croker, Ambrose	11
Collins, William	107	Crook, John	35
Collom, William	16	Crook, John	52
Colson, Francis	66	Crook, Joseph	87
Colvin, Hugh	9	Crotty, David	14
Comegys, Cornelius	58	Crowden, John	1
Connell, George	41	*Crugh, John*	11
Connell, William	86	Cubler, Jacob	103
Connelly, Patrick	106	Cullman, Adam	77
Conner, John	5	Culnan, John	93
Conner, Paul	8	Cumfort, Francis	103
Connor, John	65	Cummings, John	37
Connor, Michael	25	Cunningham, William	118
Conrad, Jacob, Junr.	3	Curry, Robert	7
Conrad, Philip	38		
Conrod, Jacob	6	Dallas, A. J.	96
Conrod, Jacob	36	Dallas, Stewart George	96
Conyngham, Frederick	118	Daller, Michael	83
Cook, George	14	Dame, Christian	52
Cook, John	22	Damm, Andrew	6
Cooper, Amanius	106	Daniel, John	5
Cope, Mathias	48	Daniel, John	10
Copple, John	11	Darrach, John	19
Corbright, John	10	Darragh, Charles	25
Cornman, John	38	Davan, John	98
Cornish, Robert	15	David, John	10
Corse, John	19	Davidson, James	70
Cottman, John	12	Davidson, Robert	11
Cottringer, James	21	Davidson, William	17
Coulthurst, Matthew	91	Davies, David	8
Comrse, Isaac	11	Davies, William	6
Coulty, Samuel	54	Davis, Isaac	69
Cove, John	88	Davis, James	93
Cowan, James	113	Davis, James	9, 39
Cowell, John	25	Davis, John	39
Cowie, Andrew	91	Davis, John	106
Cox, Jacob	29	Davis, Jonathan	95
Cox, Thomas	89	Davis, Joseph	111
Craig, Daniel	61	Davis, Peter	78
Craig, Thomas	46, 102	*Davis, (Justice)*	15
Craig, Thomas	118	Daw, John	21
Crain, Robt.	20	Day, Andrew	56
Crass, Peter	38	Deak, Thomas	60
Crawford, Charles	96	Deal, John	13
Crawford, John	112	Deamand, George	103
Crawford, Joseph	30	Dean, Conrod	90
Crawford, Samuel	10	Decoster, Charles	71
Cress, Henry	17	De Cressy, Maximilian L. A.	100
Cress, Johannes	98	De Peke, Carl	105
Crinshew, John David	70	Deering, Nicholas	73
Crispin, Peter	3	Defrancquen, Philip	111
Crispin, Samuel	51	Degenhart, Johann George	55

INDEX OF NAMES.

Name	Page	Name	Page
De Grofey, Charles	117	Ducomb, Vincent	112
De Haven, Peter	53	Dudengöss, Ludwig	82
Deimling, Frederick	88	Due, William	21
De la Croix, Joseph	99	Duffus, Andrew	113
Delaney, George	17	Duffy, James	23
Delaney, James	96	Duffy, Patrick	25
Delaplaine, James	19	Duguid, John, Junr	92
Dellap, Williams	19	Dumfield, John	9
Delonguay, Francis Moussu	91	Dan, John	113
Demd Henry	85	Dunbar, James	82
Dempsey, Barnaby	4	Dunhower, George	7
Denei, (Justice)	110	Dunlap, James	3
Denny, David	92	Dunn, Isaac B.	28
Denny, Richard	109	Dunn, Philip	115
Derry, George	89	Dunton, William	5
Desantee, Lewis	71	Durie, John	78
Deshong, Friederich	39	Darling, Joseph	5
Detterline, Henry	101	Du Simitiere, P. E.	9
Dewees, William	68	Duy, Frederick	54
Dewers, Henry	76		
Dewetter, Conrad	37	Ebalt, John	118
Dexter, James	43	Ebert, Johannes	97
Dey, Cornelius	71	Eckhart, William	49
Diamond, John	16, 39	Eckelman, Conrad	60
Dickens, Edward	12	Eckstein, Jacob	109
Dickinson, Cadr.	59	Eddleston, Lawrence	83
Dickinson, Maurice	110	Eddy, George	92
Dickson, Thomas	52	Edeling, Johann Valtin	82
Dieffenbach, Christopher Frederick	69	Egen, Leonard	6
Dill, Balthazar	82	Eggers, Nicholas	68
Dill, Nicholaus	103	Ehrenzeller, Jacob	49
Dishong, Christian	50	Eikhart, Matthias	87
Ditrich, Michael	45	*Elder, Joshua*	59
Dolby, Joseph	70	Elliott, Christopher	7
Domiller, William	43	Elliott, David	25
Donaldson & Co.	75	Elliott, Edward	18
Donnelly, Francis	23	Emory, Jabez	115
Donnelly, Terence	15	Endesruggern, Ernst	84
Donohue, John	29	Engle, Benjamin	103
Donovan, William	107	Ent, Theobald	40
Dorey, Peter Victor	101	Ermanberger, Friederich	53
Douglass, E.	109	Erringer, Jacob	3, 39
Douglass, John	11	Esenbeck, William	80
Douglass, John	88	Eshrick, George	81
Douglas, William	21	Esling, Frederick	102
Dover, Frederick	102	Esling, Nicholas	71
Dow, Benjamin	89	*Esling, Paul*	102
Dowling, Kerence	65	Evans, Caleb	101
Downey, William	92	*Evans, David*	101
Downing, Nicholas	93	Evans, Lewis	115
Downs, Robert	71	Evans, Samuel	39
Doz, Andrew	3, 52	Everhard, David	55, 101
Draper, Jonathan	3, 38	Everhart, John	55

INDEX OF NAMES.

Name	PAGE	Name	PAGE
Everly, John	17	Francis, Jacob	84
		Francis, Tench	18
Facundas, Jacob	11	Francis, Thomas	43
Fagan, Edmond	20	Frank, Isaac	99
Fajon, John	7	Frank, Jacob	17
Falkener, William	101	Franses, Peter	85
Falkenstein, Ludwig	39	Fraser, Samuel	95
Farnsworth, James	20	Frazer, John	22
Fecundas, William	57	Frichman, Johann Heinrich	86
Feel, Rudolph	64	Friedelbach, Johann	91
Fegal, John	18	Friederich, Wilhelm	9
Ferguson, Ephraim	107	Fritenheiler, Adam	90
Ferguson, Hugh	13	Fry, John	1
Ferguson, William	117	Fryhoffer, John	18
Fesmore, John	23	Fryhoffer, Wollery	18
Fians, William	7	Fuller, Benjamin	2
Field, Peter	102	Fullerton, Robert	50, 59
Finley, Francis	36	Fullerton, William	5
Finley, James	28		
Fineton, John	112	Gaa, Gilbert	110
Fisher, Andreas	9	Gaillard, Alexander	101
Fisher, George	5	Galvan, John	110
Fisher, Johannes	99	Gamble, James	63
Fisher, John	56	Ganeber, Michael	57
Fisler, Jacob	5, 36	Garaud, Jacob	102
Fite, Andrew	6	Garanger, Lewis	105
Fitzgerald, Thomas	43	Gardenok, Powel Adam	69
Fitzpatrick, John	75	Gardette, James	110
Fitzsimons, John	117	Gardner, John	3
Fleeson, Plunket	35, 15, 62	Garhart, Daniel	30
Fleeson, Thomas	40	Garman, William	77
Fleisher, Casper	12	Garrett, Adam	14
Floak, Justice	96	Garrett, Conrad	111
Flounders, Edward	48	Gebheart, Georg	51
Folk, Matthew	11	*Gebler, Godfred*	66
Folt, Daniel	24	Gehring, Michael	79
Folwell, William	20	Geiss, Everhart	2
Footman, Peter	17	Geisse, Francis	11
Ford, Christopher	114	Gentle, James	73
Ford, John	43	George, Andrew	50
Forgey, William	115	George, George	51
Forst, Abraham	68	George, John	50
Forster, C. Martin	52	George, John, Junr.	50
Forster, John	52	Gibbons, Henry	10
Forsyth, George	18	Gibbs, Josiah W.	107
Fourage, Stephen	61	Giessler, Johannes	83
Fox, George	36	Gilbert, Jacob	2
Fox, John	74	Gilbert, Jacob, Junr.	2
Fox, John George, Senr.	6	Gilchrist, Adam	22
Fox, Justinian	50	Gilchrist, James	26
Fox, Michael	11	*Gilchrist, John*	71
Foy, Matthew	43	*Gillingham, James*	62
Fraley, John	51	Gill, Josiah	8

INDEX OF NAMES. 133

	PAGE		PAGE
Gitts, Michael	51	Grisler, Frederick	13
Glick, Johann	83	Grobey, Johann	97
Glisson, William	51	Groff, Adam	40
Gloeding, Abraham	47	Grosse, (Doctr.)	96
Glyn, Patrick	116	Grotz, George	8
Godfrey, William E.	18	Grover, John	17
Godshall, John	109	Grubb, John Herbert*	73
Goette, Israel	98	Grunwold, Frederick	78
Goggin, Williams	58	*Guier, Adam*	101
Goldschmitt, Caspar	77	Guier, John	101
Gominger, Jacob	19	Guiney, William	41
Goodman, Conrod	18, 39	Guinep, William	51
Goodman, John	7	Gusse, Francis	58, 59
Goodman, John	111	Guy, John	12
Gorgas, Benjamin	5	Guy, Richard	12
Gorgas, John	5		
Gosner, Casper	58	Haas, Jacob	7
Gosner, Daniel	50	Hager, Martin	95
Gotlib, Conrad	87	Hague, Elsha	117
Gotthart, Johann Conrad	35	Hain, John	57
Govett, James	40	Haines, Michael	116
Grab, Peter	49	Halburtat, John	36
Graff, Jacob	4	Hale, Thomas	9
Graham, Matthew	107	Hall, James	35
Graham, William	23, 12	Hall, James	101
Graner, Frederic	91	Hall, Parry	96
Grant, Alexander	116	Hall, Reuben	7
Grant, Henry	93	Hall, Richard	12
Grant, Isaac	7	Hall, Thomas	36
Grant, Peter	59	Hall, Walter	15
Gratz, Michael	52	Hallam, Lewis	98
Gravel, John	43	Halling, Solomon	49
Gray, Joseph	70	Hambright, John	7
Gray, William	25	Hamel, James	25
Gray, William	67	Hamilton, Andrew	18, 18
Gray, William	70	Hamilton, Henry	91
Greble, John	48	Hamilton, John	73
Green, Nathaniel	4	Hamilton, John	88
Green, Peter	13	Hamilton, John	99
Green, Gen.	20	Hamilton, W.	38
Greenway, William	7	Hammer, Henry	92
Greenwood, Alexander	60	Hankel, Conrad	76
Greer, Charles	51	Hankel, Jacob	41
Greer, George	118	Hans, Conrad	59
Greer, Henry	99	Hansell, David	15
Gregg, Robert	29	Hansell, William	10
Greswold, Thomas	17	Hansil, Peter David	6
Greve, Henry	28	Hansman, Christian	36
Griffith, Cadwalader	117	Harar, Daniel	43
Griffith, Evan	42	Harbeson, Benjamin, Junr.	115
Griffith, William	12	Hargis, Abraham	22
Grim, Nicholas	13	Harkness, Samuel	109
Grimes, John	71	Harly, George	60

INDEX OF NAMES.

Name	Page	Name	Page
Harma, Joseph	27	Hickey, Timothy	75
Harman, George	111	Heffernan, John	51
Harman, George	111	Hillborn, Joseph	16, 11
Harman, Jacob	1	Hillborn, Miles	3
Harper, John	86	Hines, Thomas	83
Harraway, John	6	Hiney, George	12
Harris, Henry	31, 85	Hinkle, Nicholas	22
Harris, James	15, 38	Hinton, George	71
Harrison, Joseph	100	Hitchings, William Vaughan	63
Harrison, William P.	112	Hitner, Frederick	5
Hart, Christopher	10	Hodge, Andrew, Junr.	15
Hart, George	10	*Hodgkinson, Bethenah*	70
Hart, Henry	10	Hodgson, Alvery	8
Hart, Joseph	2	Hodgson, Joseph	111
Hartlau, Johan	79	Hoffer, Philip	51
Harvey, Joseph	10	Hoffner, George	26
Hasig, Valentine	10	Hoffsteller, John	11
Haussman, John D.	99	Hoggen, James	102
Havesstrick, Jonas	87	Hohnerson, Matthias	91
Hay, John	11	Holeget, Matthew	6
Hayes, Isaac	53	Holegit, John	5
Hazen, ——	26	Holland, Benjamin	19
Hazleton, Albright	60	Hollinshead, William	1
Hazleton, Josiah	13	Holmes, Abraham	8
Hazlewanger, Lewis	4	Holsten, Frederick	7
Hazlewood, John, Junr.	28	Holsten, Matthias	7
Hazley, Charles	82	Holsten, Peter	8
Healy, William	105	Homaker, Joseph	100
Heatly, Charles	76	Honeycomb, Joseph	48
Heaton, Jonathan	47	Honeyman, Samuel	59
Heinrichs, Philip	55	Honeyman, William	29
Heizer, Henry	82	Hood, Thomas	107
Heffernan, John	17	Hoofman, James	116
Heller, Johannes	10	Hook, George	68
Heller, Joseph	21	Hook, William	82
Helm, John	50	Hooker, Thomas	87
Hembel, Samuel	22	Hooper, Matthew	48
Henderich, Johan Martin	96	Horn, John	9
Henderson, John	8, 11	Horner, James	2
Henderson, William	23	Hossman, Stokely	7
Henry, John	73	Houlgate, Cornelius	6
Hertford, George	76	Honshold, Sebastian	9
Herron, James G.	26	Howell, Abraham	27
Hess, George	12	Howell, David	89
Hess, John	117	Howell, Richard	99
Hess, Nicholas	117	Huber, Georg	72
Hetherington, John	60	Hubley, Adam	1
Hettmannkerger, Frantz Wilhelm	57	*Hubley, (Justice)*	105
Heyl, George	49	Huckel, William	91
Heyl, John	10	Hudson, Henry	70
Heyneman, Heynrich	82	Hudson, James	15
Heysham, Robert	16	Hudson, John	110
Hibberd, Joseph	17, 18	Hufty, Simon	12

INDEX OF NAMES. 135

	PAGE		PAGE
Huggins, George	89	Johnston, Robert	113
Hugh, William	106	Jonasson, Neels	7
Hughes, John	66	Jones, David	1
Hull, (Justice)	47	Jones, Francis	19, 42
Humphreys, Benjamin	49	Jones, George Buch	90
Humphreys, James	13	Jones, Israel	17
Humphreys, Samuel	53	Jones, Jesse	16
Humphreys, Thomas	18	Jones, John	24
Hunn, John	26	Jones, Joshua	17
Hunt, Gilbert	90	JONES, PAUL	28
Hunt, Richard	38	Jones, William	5
Hunt, William	57	Jones, William	16, 36
Hunter, Charles	98	Jordan, Joseph	116
Huntheimer, Tictus	87	Jude, Frederick	101
Hurley, Thomas	114	Junkin, Samuel	42
Hurry, Arthur	15	Jutter, Johann Christopher	35
Hurst, James	73		
Huston, Edward	64	Kaje, Augustus	80
Hutman, Peter	11	Katz, Heinrich	53
Huvort, Loedwick	98	Katz, Henry	7
Hyneman, Frederick	115	Kauch, Christian	81
Hyneman, Henry	11	Kaworth, John	25
Hynes, Brian	71	Keating, Luke	35
Hysmmingle, Nicholas	12	Keavort, Christian	81
		Keble, John	4
Ilgen, Lewis	80	Keeling, John Hignet	52
Ingiez, Jerom	49	Keen, Joseph	103
Inglis, George	71	Keene, L.	28
Ioane, Marcus	68	Keichler, John	38
Ironning, George	11	Keidel, George	78
Irwin, Robert	6	Keisler, Jacob	9
Irwin, Thomas	38	Keller, Conrad	69
Isaac, Charles	70	Kelley, James	50
Isinhoot, Andrew	13	Kelly, John	4
Israel, Israel	110	Kelly, William	94
		Kelsey, Joshua	89
Jackson, James	79	Kemble, Peter	76
Jackson, John M.	20	Kemble, William	13
Jackson, Thomas	85	Kemmel, Peter	90
Jackson, William	16	Kendall, Joseph	5
Jacobs, Nicholas	3	Kenedy, John	75
Jagger, Abraham	88	Kennedy, Robert	22
James, Benjamin	113	*Kephard, Coron*	60
Jamison, John	26	Keram, Edward	1
Janus, George	8	Kerlin, John, Junr.	51
Jarvis, Jacob	76	Kesler, Henry	105
Jeffery, William	19	Kessler, Leonard	20
Jervis, John	67	Keys, John	13
Jewell, Robert	2	Keyser, John	75
Johner, Georg	66	Kidd, William	3
Johnson, John	108	Killamer, Hance	84
Johnston, James	97	Kimhel, Heinrich	52
Johnston, John	22	Kinder, Gottlieb	100

INDEX OF NAMES.

Name	PAGE	Name	PAGE
King, Abraham	75	Lang, Thomas	112
King, Isaac	73	Langdale, Samuel	3, 39
King, James	106	Langrall, Levin	21
Kingsfield, Wendell	4	Laodie, John Claude	95
Kinkead, James	50	Larrison, George	72
Kinnard, Jacob	41	Latch, Jacob	36
Kinnear, James	17	Latch, Rudolph	8
Kinsel, John	117	Lauer, Philip	27
Kintzing, Abraham, Junr.	107	Laughlin, Jacob	7
Kipp, Andreas	83	Lavisyler, Thomas	28
Kirk, Anthony	47	Lawrence, John	51
Kirk, James	21	Lawrence, William	3
Kirkbride, (Col.)	53	Lawrence, William	56
Kirkhoff, Christian	12	Lawson, John	15
Kirwan, Nicholas	73	Lawyer, Christian	18
Klein, Johan	79	Laycock, John	94
Klein, Philip	29	Leaman, Joseph	3
Knight, Charles	16	Lear, John	12
Knoepler, George	67	Lear, John L.	65
Knoll, Ludwick	18, 39	Leavering, Benjamin	1
Knowles, John	83	Lechler, Adam	58
Knox, Francis	29	Ledra, Joseph	20
Knox, Hugh	20	Leech, Isaac	20
Knox, Mathew	55	Leech, Peter	80
Koehler, Bernhard	79	Leech, Robert	12
Koehler, John Adam	59	Lehré, Jacob	50
Koehnle, John	51	Leib, Michael	17
Köhr, Philip	82	Leitshok, Conrad	87
Kook, John	35	Lemaigre, Pierre	64
Kooper, Georg	106	Lemaire, Jean Baptiste	113
Kooper, George	46	Lemau, Andrew	9
Korloder, Friederich	88	Lennerd, John	45
Korn, Gabriel	12	Lentz, Heinrich	9
Koy, William	79	*Lentz, Henry*	101
Krafst, Michael	61	Lentz, John	101
Kreaning, Francis	76	Leonard, Joseph	40
Kresson, Joseph	111	Lesh, Zachariah	97
Kromer, Leonard	2	Letchworth, John	101
Krop, Jean	100	Letts, Michael	15
Kubler, Martin	108	Levering, Abraham	2
Kugler, Christopher	28	Levering, Jacob	8
Kunze, John C.	36	Levering, William	102
Kurtz, George	36	*Levering, William*	102
Kurtz, Peter	17	Levy, Eleazer	18
		Lewis, John	79
Lackrum, John	108	Lewis, Joseph	54
Lahm, Jacob	98	Lewis, Pearce	12
Lake, Richard	105	Liberstin, Felix	51
Lake, Thomas	23	Ligaux, Peter	112
Lake, Capt. Thomas	23	Light, James	56
Lake, William	11	Light, Peter	16
Lambeth, Joseph	109	Lincoln, James	64
Landerken, Patrick	74	Linnard, William	65

INDEX OF NAMES. 137

Name	PAGE	Name	PAGE
Linniberger, John	53	Macpherson, William	91
Lint, Frederick	53	Maffett, Joseph	108
Linton, John	55	Maher, Martin	97
Lippee, John	11	Makemson, George	47
Lipsey, Henry	30	Malone, John	10
Lisle, Joseph	11	Malone, Peter	67
Litchenham, Jacob	39	Mandry, Richard	81
Llewelyn, John	19	Maner, Julius	117
Llewelyn, Morriss	19	Mansai, Nicola	113
Loardan, Charles	11	Marcer, Benjamin James	72
Lockhart, William	103	Marcus, Johannes	70
Lockwood, James	29	Markoe, Peter	99
Lodge, John	5	Marks, Levy	3
Logan, Charles	15	Marsan, John	97
Loge, John	26	Marshal, Anthony	71
Lohman, William	13	Martin, Hugh	26
Lohra, John	20	Martin, John	46
Long, John	43	Martin, William	27
Loomsbach, Johannes	76	Mathes, John	49
Lorden, Charles	60	Mathias, Joseph	19
Lorden, George	43	MATLACK, TIMOTHY	2, 73
Lotie, Laurence	117	Matlack, William	3, 36
Loughlin, (Squire)	107	Mattson, Israel	63
Louriette, Zachariah	105	Matzinger, George	42
Loving, Casper	64	Matzinger, John	7
Lowden, Jacob	111	Maur, Jacob	53
Lownes, Joseph	19	May, John	89
Lowrey, Samuel	108	Mayer, George	26
Loxly, Benjamin, Junr.	1	*Mayer, Jacob*	26
Lubrer, Adrien Joseph	113	Mayer, Johannes	72
Lucas, James	11	*Mayland, (Col.)*	66
Ludgate, Richard	15, 53	Maynard, Joseph	73
Lumsden, Robert	116	Maysey, Thomas	110
Lutch, Jacob	6	McAlestor, John	18
Luther, Conrod	92	McAnally, Henry	30
Luts, Christian	66	McCall, David	111
Lutz, Conrad	4	McCarter, Charles	25
Lutz, Johann	83	McCarter, Daniel	95
Luy, Hoyman	46	McCartney, John	10
Luzer, John Andrew	92	McCarty, Marks	89
Lynch, John	111	McCary, Daniel	63
Lynch, John Patrick	68	McCausland, Marcus	71
Lynn, Jeremiah	19	McCausland, Robert	71
Lyon, Philip	91	McClarey, Archibald	23
Lyon, Samuel	3	McClatchie, William	50
Lyons, James	63	McClenney, Thomas	76
Lytle, Andrew	26	McClentick, Matthew	29
		McCollin, Andrew	59
Maag, Jacob	14	McCotter, James	6
Mackay, James	111	McCrea, Fergus	77
Mackenzie, William	19	McCulley, Thomas	104
Macky, John	2	McCulloh, John	6
Macombe, James	96	McDermott, William	109

S

138   INDEX OF NAMES.

	PAGE		PAGE
McDonald, Alexander	108	Metzinger, Michael	3
McDonald, Donald	101	Mevins, Henry	71
McDonald, William	81	Meyer, Joseph	9
McDonnell, Edward	40	Meyland, Siméon	65
McDowell, Thomas	4, 49	Middlehauser, Friederich	80
McElroy, Benjamin	110	Midwinter, John	89
McElvain, William	38	Miers, Christopher	50
McFarland, Kennedy	92	Miller, Andrew	23
McFarlane, John	11	Miller, Benjamin	48
McGee, Henry	8	Miller, Caspar	83
McGill, James	1	Miller, Christopher	46
McGouen, John	93	Miller, Henry	95
McGregor, John	79	Miller, Jacob	102
McGregor, Richard	78	Miller, Johan Georg	36
McGuire, Matthew	25	Miller, John	15
Mellench, John	30	Miller, John	81
McIntire, Andrew	12	Miller, John	93
McIntire, Thomas	28	Miller, Magnus	95
McIntosh, Donald	55	Miller, Martin	7
McIntosh, John	99	Miller, Nicholas	11
McKendrick, Archibald	39	Miller, Robert	15
McKennan, John	51	Miller, William	14
McKenzie, William Jackson	106	Miller, William	95
McKiernan, Charles	116	Miller, William	103
McKim, John	4	Mills, John	15
McKinsey, John	111	Mingle, John	117
McLean, Daniel	21	Mitchel, John	56
McLean, James	25	Mitchell, Hugh	10
McLean, Keneth	78	Mitchell, John	29
McMahon, Michael	88	Mits, John Conrad	101
McMichael, William	46	Molineux, Frederick	98
McMillen, James	77	Montgomery, Daniel	74
McMullen, James	80	Montgomery, Duncan	110
McMullen, Michael	20	Montgomery, James	23
McNachtane, John	74	Montgomery, William	31
McNair, John	11	Moore, Bartholomew	2
McSparran, William	9	Moore, George	65
McVeagh, Benjamin	56	Moore, George	106
Meade, George	97	Moore, Hugh	76
Mears, John	91	Moore, J.	27
Meayn, Ludwig	80	Moore, John	11
Mellen, Peter	41	Moore, John	75
Mellenberger, Peter	13	Moore, Philip	21
Mellor, Johann Xhart	64	Moore, Robert	41
Melvin, Robert	81	Moore, Robert K.	115
Mentges, Philip	27	Moore, William	37*
Mentz, Jomel	91	Moore, William	43
Mercier, Joseph	101	Moore, (Justice)	60
Meridith, Charles	16	Morgan, John	51
Mervine, Andrew	4	Morgan, Thomas	17
Mesnard, Thomas	63	Morgan, Thomas	12
Metay, William	11	Morrell, Robert	27, 97
Metts, Adam	13	Morris, Evan	9

INDEX OF NAMES. 139

Name	Page	Name	Page
Morris, Luke, Junr.	21	Oliver, George	73
Morris, Thomas A.	104	O'Neill, Alexander Louis	69
Morrison, Daniel	11	O'Neill, Thomas	106
Morton, George	8	Opperman, Adam	77
Morton, Israel	7	Ord, John	49
Moser, George	14	Organ, John	30
Moylan, Jasper Alexander	70	Orner, Michael	2
Moylan, John	70	Osmos, Henry	91
Moyston, Edward	106	Oswald, Eleazer	23
Müller, Christian	81	Oswald, Robert	113
Müller, Johannes	55	Otenkerken, John	17
Müller, Michael	15	Ott, Peter	21
Murdaugh, James	48	Otto, Francis	77
Murgatroyd, John	10	Otto, Johannes	83
Murphy, Alexander	93	Overly, John	38
Murphy, Thomas	74	Overstake, Christian	56
Murry, Jeremiah	74	Owens, Patrick	25
Mussi, Joseph	114	Owens, William	115
Muster, John	83		
Myers, Henry	81	Packer, James	40
Myrtelus, Adam	3	Paisley, Robert	114
		Paleske, Charles	105
		Palmer, John	16, 46
Naer, David	66	Palmer, Joseph	18, 49
Nassau, John	96	Palmer, Thomas	41
Naffets, Edward	63	Pancoast, David	18
Neill, James	37	Panrert, Johann	64
Nesbit, J. M.	2	Parker, Richard	106
Nevell, Thomas	6	Parkes, Joseph	45
Nevil, James	96	Parkhill, Andrew	63
Newark, Thomas	73	Parkhill, John	13
Newel, David	116	Parkmann, Johannes	77
Nice, John	59	*Paschal, Benjamin*	48
Nice, Lewis	62	Paschall, Benjamin	2
Nicholas, William	54	Paschall, Benjamin	8
Nicol, Robert	112	Paschall, Thomas	44
Nicholson, John	113	Patterson, John	35
Niemond, Johann	89	Pattison, Robert	21
Nimmo, Alexander	101	Patton, John	27
Nixon, John	2	Patton, William	26
Nolbrow, William	15	Paul, David	6
Nouveller, Matthias	37	Paul, Jonathan	6
Norton, William	29	Peale, James	18
Nourse, Joseph	68	Pearson, Joshua	20
Nuff, Melchoir	40	Peiss, George	53
Nugent, Edmond	18, 46	Pelozi, Vicenzo Maria	100
Nugent, James	65	Peltz, Philip	103
		Pemberton, Handy	106
O'Donnell, Patrick	75	Pemberton, Joseph	46
Oellers, James	46	Pendleton, Solomon	95
Ogden, John	24	Penington, Daniel	110
Ogden, Joseph, Junr.	61, 64	Penrose, Isaac	19
Oilt, Henry	92	Penrose, Samuel	17, 48

INDEX OF NAMES.

Name	Page	Name	Page
Perkins, William	66	Pugh, Henry	19
Perree, Nicholas	64	Pugh, William	36
Perret, Henry	13	*Pulaski, Count*	69
Perry, Richard	73		
Peterman, Christian	17	Quain, John	14
Peters, Garrett	26	Queerfort, Henry	90
Peters, Capt. John	58	Quest, Nicholas	54
Peters, Samuel	17	Quin, Jeremiah	57
Peters, William, Junr.	74	Quinlen, John	97
Pettit, Charles	23		
Pettit, Thomas	72	Rambo, Peter	16
Phelps, Matthew	22	Randall, Thomas	108
Phile, Charles	50	Ranganer, Jacob	79
Phile, John	23	Rasbotham, James	41
Phillips, John	100	Ratzner, George	18
Pierie, Martin	53	Read, George	76
Pigeon, Conrad	12	Read, James	2
Pigisson, John	95	Read, John	28
Pine, Lazarus	6	Read, Samuel	75
Pine, Robert E.	113	Rede, Zeman Thomas	98
Pinkerton, William	105	Reed, Christopher	58
Pinton, William	46	Reed, Francis	81
Pittman, Zacarius	85	REED, JOSEPH	2
Plack, Friederich	37	Rees, James	114
Plain, Felix	85	Reffert, Philip	6
Platt, Daniel	93	Reid, Christopher	44
Pleiney, John	70	*Reidezel.* ——	95
Plunket, Robert	42	Reiley, John, Junr.	41
Pollard, John	59	Reiley, Patrick	65
Pollock, Oliver	116	Reinbott, Christian Friederich	81
Pool, Edward	28	*Reinhard, Martin*	101
Porter, David	25	Reinhard, Peter	101
Porter, John	17	Reinhart, George	60
Porter, John	50	Remender, Peter	39
Pot, Mattis	60	Renno, Jacob	45
Poth, Adam, Junr.	57	Renshaw, Thomas	47
Poth, Johannes	57	Reshong, David	61
Powell, Anthony	81	Rey, Andrew	30
Powell, Lawrence	19	Rey, Jean Louis	15
Powell, Peter	55	Reynhart, Francis	77
Powell, William	13	Reynard, John	78
Power, Alexander	25	Rhea, John	27
Prescott, Roger	101	Rice, John	13
Presuhn, Heinrich	88	Rice, Joseph	25
Price, Edward	8	Rice, Nicholas	42
Price, Joseph	5	Richards, David	41
Price, Lewis	82	Richards, John, Junr.	112
Price, Rees	19, 37	Richards, William	7
Price, Richard	38	Richardson, William	109
Prichard, William	65	Richie, Edward	38
Pride, James	105	Richhowser, John	84
Pritchett, Rowland	67	Richman, Thomas	57
Pritner, Philip	17	Rickneal, Jacob	21

INDEX OF NAMES. 141

Name	Page	Name	Page
Riddle, David	19	Rundleman, John	86
Riddle, John	52	Rush, William	7
Ried, John	12	Rusk, William	10
Riffets, Edward	55	Russegue, Timothy	79
Rigg, Robert	7	Russell, Alexander	28
Righter, Daniel	2	Russell, James	5, 40
Righter, John	2	Rutherford, John	13
Righter, John	2	Rutter, George	61
Righter, John	35	Ryan, Edward	80
Righter, Michael	2	Ryan, James	108
Rinaldi, Charles	94	Ryan, Timothy	109
Ritgie, John	89	Ryan, Thomas	113
Ritiger, Johannes	9		
RITTENHOUSE, DAVID	6, 99	Sadler, John	102
Ritter, Charles	52	Sainton, John	112
Robert, John	80	Saldrich, David	49
Roberts, Abraham	60	Sallier, Jacque	112
Roberts, Algernon	16	Saltar, Richard	4
Roberts, James	110	Sample, Thomas	88
Roberts, John	9, 42	Sauder, Caspar	2
Roberts, William	90	Saunders, William	39
Robinett, Joseph	59	Sautter, Johannes	87
Robinson, James	86	Savage, Darby	39
Robinson, Richard	40	Savett, Henry	14
Robinson, William	36	Savidge, John	29
Robinson, William	41	Saxton, Jared	50
Robson, Robert	52	Scheiler, Johann	80
Rogers, Benjamin	101	Schin, Conrad	61
Rogers, Isabella	70	Schlosser, George	7
Rogers, James	58	Schmidt, Caspar	94
Ronals, James	77	Schmitt, Heinrich	69
Roney, James	107	Schmitt, Johannes	67
Roof, John	99	Schmitt, Valentin	76
Rose, Peter	8	Schmyser, Michael	53
Rose, William	7	Schneider, Christian	7
Rosenberger, Godfrey	80	Schneider, George	11
Ross, GEORGE	5	Schneider, Johan	92
Ross, Hugh	39	Schrack, Jacob	63
Rossiter, Thomas, Junr.	48	Schreiner, Jacob	6
Roth, Philip	5	Schunel, Baltus	80
Rothbottom, James	12	Schwalbah, Henry	1
Rothmann, Johann	74	Schwallach, Heinrich	55
Rone, Thomas	41	Scot, Robert	25
Rouking, John	6	Scott, Thomas	2
Roun, Conrad	110	Scott, William	94
Rowand, Jacob	8	Scravendyke, Peter	107
Rudolph, Christian	49	Scull, Benjamin	51
Rudolph, George	114	Scully, Barnaby	30
Rudolph, Tobias	49	*Sears, Lemuel*	22
Rudolph, Wilhelm	96	Seddon, Thomas	106
Rue, Joseph	63	Seegez, Frederick	3
Rumble, Philip	3	Seitz, John Adam	98
Rumel, Georg	83	Seixas, Abraham	23

			PAGE				PAGE
Sellers, David	.	.	50	Sink, George	.	.	12
Sellers, John, Junr.	.	.	107	Sinket, Daniel	.	.	89
Sellers, Joseph	.	.	4, 43	Sisson, Thomas	.	.	115
Sellers, Xn.	.	.	36	Sitzdorff, Wilhelm	.	.	94
Semple, Alexander	.	.	72	Skellorn, Richard	.	.	58
Semple, John	.	.	85	Sleigh, Christian	.	.	51
Serre, François	.	.	112	Sloan, William	.	.	16
Shagert, Bernhard	.	.	87	Smallwood, Peter	.	.	11
Shaller, Conrad	.	.	9	Smaltz, Heinrich	.	.	11
Shaper, John	.	.	14	Smith, Benjamin	.	.	23
Sharp, Andrew	.	.	5	Smith, Benjamin H.	.	.	114
Sharp, Jacob	.	.	5	Smith, Christopher	.	.	115
Sharswood, George	.	.	35	Smith, Daniel	.	.	95
Shaw, Daniel	.	.	12	Smith, George	.	.	115
Shaw, George	.	.	54	Smith, Hosea	.	.	21
Shaw, Patrick	.	.	29	Smith, Jacob	.	.	14
Shee, John	.	.	76	Smith, Jacob	.	.	62
Sheldon, Isaac	.	.	22	Smith, James	.	.	68
Shelvough, William	.	.	86	Smith, John	.	.	5
Shetler, Martin	.	.	95	Smith, John	.	.	28
Shetzline, Adam	.	.	66	Smith, John	.	.	37
Shields, John	.	.	94	*Smith, John*	.	.	60
Shiell, William, M.D	.	.	64	Smith, John Erdman	.	.	16
Shilling, Michael	.	.	13	Smith, Jonathan	.	.	13
Shisler, Godfrey	.	.	17, 53	Smith, Jonathan, Junr.	.	.	115
Shiver, Michael	.	.	54	Smith, Joseph	.	.	13
Shlotman, Alexander	.	.	95	Smith, Matthew	.	.	2
Shmid, Friederich	.	.	92	Smith, Michael	.	.	3
Sholtz, Martin Henry	.	.	95	Smith, Philip	.	.	21, 78
Shoster, Henry	.	.	8	Smith, Robert	.	.	97
Shove, John Albert	.	.	86	*Smith, Robert*	.	.	101
Shreiber, Jacob	.	.	86	Smith, Robert, Junr.	.	.	101
Shrive, Samuel	.	.	59	Smith, Samuel	.	.	64
Shriver, Joseph	.	.	4	Smith, Thomas	.	.	17
Shubert, Michael	.	.	5	Smith, Thomas	.	.	67
Shuchard, Peter	.	.	85	Smith, William	.	.	91
Shuder, Ludwick	.	.	60	Smith, William	.	.	110
Shughart, Johannes	.	.	96	Smith, William Austin	.	.	71
Shuman, Friederich	.	.	86	*Smithson, (Justice)*	.	.	20
Sibley, Jacob	.	.	24	Smock, Robert	.	.	26
Sibley, Rudolph	.	.	8, 38	Sneider, Benedict	.	.	60
Sicard, Stephen	.	.	100	Snelhart, John	.	.	65
Sickard, Georg David	.	.	16	Sneling, George	.	.	15
Sieman, Waldrop	.	.	78	Snyder, George	.	.	55
Sim, Robert	.	.	93	Snyder, John	.	.	111
Simes, Samuel	.	.	108	Solter, John	.	.	15
Simmons, Thomas	.	.	66	Soly, Alexander	.	.	18
Simon, Johan Barnard	.	.	67	Sothern, William	.	.	116
Simons, Stephen	.	.	46	Sonder, Casper	.	.	47
Sims, Bartholomew	.	.	102	Sowersby, William	.	.	41
Sinter, John	.	.	118	Soytler, Gotfred	.	.	80
Sinclton, Richard	.	.	42	Spalter, John	.	.	85
Sink, Abraham	.	.	16	Sparks, Henry	.	.	73

www.ingramcontent.com/pod-product-compliance
Lightning Source LLC
Chambersburg PA
CBHW070302230426
43664CB00014B/2609